## DEDICATION

For Mary

# TABLE OF ILLUSTRATIONS

# THE BIRDS
# OF
# QUETICO PROVINCIAL PARK
# AND
# THE ATIKOKAN AREA

.

## D A V I D   H.   E L D E R

*Friends of Quetico Park*

Leech Printing Ltd.
Brandon, Manitoba, Canada

# TABLE OF CONTENTS

## ACKNOWLEDGEMENTS

This book on the birds of Quetico Provincial Park and the Atikokan area would not have been possible without the generous support of "The Friends of Quetico Park". In particular, John Pringle acted as an advisor, editor and critic and Diana Ellieff assisted with word processing, both with limitless patience and consideration.

Gisela Ewald created the line drawings that illustrate the book. The excellent quality of her work is self-evident.

Many people, both birders and non-birders, have contributed to the cumulative total of information on birds in Quetico Provincial Park and the Atikokan area. Shirley Peruniak, park historian and naturalist, has ensured the wealth of data is organized, current and available for general use. Her efforts are deeply appreciated.

My wife, Mary, took on the seemingly endless job of processing the initial drafts of this book. Her patience, understanding and support made the finished publication possible.

## PREFACE

Birds are an obvious part of the "Quetico Experience" and a constant source of attraction and enjoyment. Even the most "tuned-out" park visitor will see and hear birds. A soaring eagle, a calling loon or the magical appearance of Gray Jays at meal time, catch and hold one's attention. Even without proper identification, birds will help shape one's impressions of the park as much as the weather, the scenery, the trees and plants, the animals and fish.

This publication is not intended to serve as a field guide or identification manual to the birds of Quetico. There are several excellent books presently available that fill this need. It is intended to give those park visitors interested in birds some idea of what species they may expect to see during their stay and where they may expect to see them. The author hopes the book will fan a spark and open the world of birds and birding to new enthusiasts.

# THE BIRDS OF QUETICO PROVINCIAL PARK AND THE ATIKOKAN AREA

## Introduction

Quetico Provincial Park is a 475,780 hectare wilderness park located in Northwestern Ontario, 160 kilometres west of Thunder Bay.

The park, with its myriad of interconnected lakes, provides wilderness canoeing opportunities that are unparalleled in North America.

Prehistoric man wandered through Quetico as early as 12,500 years ago, and, as evidenced by bits of broken pottery and stone tool flakes, camped on many of the sites used by canoeists today. A rich history including the fur trade and the western settlement era further illustrates the significance and importance of the area.

First declared a forest reserve in 1909, Quetico became a park in 1913. Although use of the park was light, it quickly gained a reputation as a wilderness area which it holds to this day. Each year 25,000 canoeists travel the water routes and enjoy the aesthetics, the history and the flora and fauna.

Closely associated with the town of Atikokan (population 4,200), the park is a major tourist attraction and the town is quickly becoming known as the Canoeing Capital of Canada.

# Geology

    Quetico Provincial Park lies within the southern portion of a vast ancient formation known as the Precambrian Shield or the Canadian Shield. The Shield forms the foundation of the North American Continent and consists of some of the oldest rocks on earth. Created during the Archean age, these rocks were last affected by a major period of mountain building about 2,500 million years ago. Metavolcanics form the source material of the park and were probably formed 2,700 million years ago.

    The formidable age of the rocks in Quetico and the erosive effect of eons of wear by wind, water and ice have resulted in a low rolling topography that was already established prior to the last glaciers. Their advance and retreat shaped the face of today's Quetico, characterized by frequent outcroppings of bare bedrock and a general northeast-southwest alignment of lakes. Two ridges of sand and gravel up to 50 metres deep trend northwest-southeast in the northeastern corner of the park, the result of debris accumulating at the edge of a stabilized glacier front. The southern half of the park exhibits a more broken topography and the long narrow lakes possess some spectacular rock cliffs.

# Drainage

    Water is the very heart and soul of Quetico. The

ancient drainage channels were completely disrupted by the actions of the great ice sheets. As the glacial ice sheets retreated, excess water tended to spill over the lowest points on the shorelines of newly-formed lakes. The result is the haphazard drainage pattern that now characterizes Quetico, with waters flowing in all directions of the compass. Ultimately all Quetico waters drain to the west, through Rainy Lake to Lake of the Woods, Lake Winnipeg and eventually to Hudson Bay.

## Climate

Quetico and the Atikokan area have a somewhat warmer and drier climate than the rest of Northern Ontario which is generally influenced by the continental polar air mass. This moderated climate is a result of the influence of the continental dry air mass from the foothills of the Rockies which tends to decrease humidity and increase evaporation and transpiration. Because temperature isotherms trend from the northwest to the southeast, the July mean daily temperature of Quetico is equal to that of Gravenhurst in south-central Ontario. A precipitation mean of 69 cm. compared to 86 cm. for Toronto reflects the decreasing trend in the province from east to west. Almost 30 percent of the annual precipitation for the area comes during the months of July and August.

Mean temperatures range from 19.0 deg. C. in July to -16.7 deg. C. in January.

# Flora

    The climatic conditions of Quetico and the Atikokan area have a profound effect on the local flora. Quetico occupies a zone of transition between the Great Lakes-St. Lawrence Forest (mixed forest) to the south, the Boreal Forest to the north, and the Great Plains to the west and the south-west. Boreal species tend to predominate, characterized by Jack Pine, Black Spruce, White Birch and Trembling Aspen. In the nutrient-poor acidic soils overlaying granite, the understorey vegetation is almost exclusively boreal. Leatherleaf, Labrador Tea, Sphagnum and a dozen or so other hardy northern species recur somewhat monotonously.

    Mixed forest species are found sporadically throughout the park. Being at the edge of their range, these species are restricted to sites of hotter-than-normal micro-climate on south-facing slopes, rocky ridge tops, lake shores and islands, especially where richer, less acidic soils are present. Red Pine and White Pine, species so characteristic of the shorelines and skylines of Quetico, appear to be much more abundant than they actually are due to their habit of growing in extensive and almost pure stands along shorelines and ridges. Other mixed forest species such as Yellow Birch, White Elm, Red Maple, Silver Maple and Red Ash occur sporadically and minimally. Shrubs and plants of a more southern nature include Hawthorn, Poison Ivy, Stinging Nettle, Bittersweet, Jack-in-the-Pulpit and Blunt-lobed Hepatica.

    Evidence of the western influence on the flora of the

area includes components of no fewer than three Great Plains forests. These are: Basswood from the dry humid mid-western United States, Red Oak from the sub-humid mid-Mississippi area and Bur Oak-Aspen from sub-humid Manitoba. Again the western species tend to be confined to the richer-soiled, hotter and drier sites in the park. Shrubs and herbs belonging to this western association include Smooth Sumac, Alum Root, Freshwater Cord Grass and just 32 km. west of the park on islands in Rainy Lake, Prickly Pear Cactus.

Fire and logging have exerted a strong influence on the present forest cover of Quetico. Because of its drier climate, this region is more susceptible to outbreaks of fire than is much of the remainder of Ontario. Approximately 50 percent of the park area has been burned over in the last 100 years. The forests of Quetico again reflect their boreal character in that they are essentially fire perpetuated.

## Fauna

The coniferous forests of Quetico provide suitable habitats for a wide variety of animals. Beaver, Red Squirrel and Eastern Chipmunk are the most frequently observed animals. Although Pine Marten, Mink, Otter and the Long-tailed Weasel are rather common, it is unusual to see them because of their secretive nature. Of the larger animals, Black Bear, Moose, White-tailed Deer and the Timber Wolf are occasionally observed by lucky canoeists. The park has seven species of frogs, one species of toad, and two species each of salamander, snake and turtle.

# Ornithological Work in Quetico Provincial Park and the Atikokan Area

There is no indication that any formal ornithological studies have been carried out in the area. Park naturalists in Quetico have, over the years, retained records of species observed in the park and evidence of breeding. A card system is kept up to date at the Visitor Services Headquarters at French Lake. All park records are based on sight observations and the occasional specimen obtained as a result of accidental death. Park naturalists who have contributed to the knowledge of Quetico's birds include Dan Strickland, Bruce Thacker, Doug Haddow, Alan Wormington, Shan Walshe and Shirley Peruniak.

Outside Quetico, systemic work on birds is again almost non-existent. Over the years individuals living in Atikokan, having an interest in birds, have retained personal sight records. Dr. G. W. Kristjanson kept personal records for many years and is still an active birder. Shirley Peruniak, another long-time Atikokan resident, has kept records of birds of the area and published an annotated list of 197 species in The Ontario Field Biologist. The list includes many unique records, such as Varied Thrush, Mountain Bluebird and Lark Sparrow, all visitors from the west. Peruniak also initiated the Atikokan Christmas Bird Census in 1960 and the Breeding Bird Census in 1968. Both of these censuses are continued today. Peruniak's work is certainly the most consistent material available.

Since 1973 other individuals interested in birds have contributed significant sight and breeding records. These include Tom Nash, Nancy Bray, Don Graham and the author.

At the present time a total of 252 species of birds has been recorded in Quetico and the Atikokan area. Of these, 139 have been known to breed.

## Habitat and Birds

While most of Quetico Park and the Atikokan area can be classified as forested land, it is by no means uniform. A wide variety of forest conditions exist, each with its own characteristic tree and plant species, age and composition. Some, such as a mature stand of Jack Pine or an open Black Spruce bog, may contain only one major tree species. Others, such as an immature mixed-wood forest, may have six to eight predominant deciduous and coniferous trees growing in dense profusion. Forests are complex systems with many interactions among plants, animals, soils and climate.

Birds seek out and use specific habitats that best meet their particular needs to ensure the continuance of the species. Being adaptable and mobile is essential to a given species to allow survival when it is out of its "preferred habitat", such as during migration.

In an attempt to assist birders in the area, a number of habitats will be described, accompanied by a list of bird species usually found therein. The bird list is by no means complete and is only intended to give an indication of what species will most likely be encountered.

# Lakes

The lakes and streams of Quetico and the Atikokan area are a major feature of the boreal environment. To the canoeist, lakes are a source of wilderness recreation and provide the easiest means of transportation through a land that would be almost inaccessible without them.

Birds encountered on the larger lakes are few in number but tend to be large and even spectacular, such as the Bald Eagle. Small pine-clad islands, commonly found in the area lakes, should be checked for breeding Merlins. This small falcon appears to favour islands as nesting sites.

The primary species found in this habitat include:

| | |
|---|---|
| Common Loon | Osprey |
| Great Blue Heron | Bald Eagle |
| Mallard | Broad-winged Hawk |
| American Black Duck | Spotted Sandpiper |
| Common Goldeneye | Herring Gull |
| Common Merganser | Belted Kingfisher |
| Turkey Vulture | |

During the spring and fall migrations, the lakes are used by nearly all the species of waterfowl recorded for the area.

Lake and Island Habitat

# Woodland Ponds

This habitat is very common in Quetico and is usually the result of beaver activity. The ponds vary greatly in size and in the amount of open water they contain. As a result they are very rich in bird life, attracting many species that are not found in continuous forest. Surrounded by forest, they are excellent birding sites. The observer can sit quietly in one place and in the course of a couple of hours see many of the species living on and around the pond. In addition, the patient observer may see Moose, White-tailed Deer, Otter and Mink. Recently-flooded areas may contain numerous dead and dying trees; older ones only a few remnant stubs. Accordingly, the bird life of the pond varies with the age of the pond.

Species characteristic of the woodland pond habitat include:

| | |
|---|---|
| Great Blue Heron | Olive-sided Flycatcher |
| American Black Duck | Tree Swallow |
| Mallard | Northern Waterthrush |
| Ring-necked Duck | Common Yellowthroat |
| Hooded Merganser | Song Sparrow |
| Broad-winged Hawk | Lincoln's Sparrow |
| Solitary Sandpiper(migration) | Swamp Sparrow |
| Spotted Sandpiper | Red-winged Blackbird |
| Belted Kingfisher | Rusty Blackbird (rare) |

The small ponds also attract a variety of migrating waterfowl during the spring and fall seasons.

Woodland Pond Habitat

## Cutover and Burned Areas

Although the effects of logging operations and fire are devastating to the resident birdlife found in these areas, healing soon starts. A whole new habitat is created and is quickly utilized by birds that enjoy more open surroundings. As the forest slowly replaces itself it goes through a series of successional stages. Trees and shrubs intolerant to shading pioneer the site and, as they grow upward, an understorey of more tolerant species follows.

With the exception of the northeastern corner of Quetico, the discernible effects of logging are few. The old logging methods using horses and manpower were mainly aimed at White and Red Pine and were essentially selective. The impact on a given area was considerably less than the effect of modern mechanized practices. Outside Quetico, cutovers of all ages can be found throughout the district, each with its bird life reflective of the successional stage of forest regrowth.

Much of the park has been burned in the past. Some fires consumed thousands of forested acres before dying out. Since the 1940's, fire detection and suppression techniques have resulted in a great reduction of major fires and most recent burns in the park have been quite small.

The following species favour the open and immature forest conditions created by logging activities and fire:

Red-tailed Hawk          Cedar Waxwing
American Kestrel          Red-eyed Vireo

Ruffed Grouse
Northern Hawk Owl (rare)
Common Nighthawk
Three-toed Woodpecker
Black-backed Woodpecker
Northern Flicker
Eastern Kingbird
Tree Swallow
Veery

Chestnut-sided Warbler
Mourning Warbler
American Redstart
Common Yellowthroat
Indigo Bunting
  (occasional)
White-throated Sparrow
American Goldfinch
American Robin

Cutover and Burned Area Habitat

## **Open Black Spruce Bog**

These areas are another easily-identified characteristic habitat of the northern boreal forest. Spruce bogs are extremely interesting, not only for birds but also for plants and insects, particularly butterflies. The bogs can be quite large but most are under 40 hectares in size. As implied by their name, the bogs are sparsely treed, with the main species being stunted Black Spruce and the occasional Tamarack. Shrub growth may be quite dense but is usually low and includes Labrador Tea, Leatherleaf, Bog Laurel, Bog Rosemary and Dwarf Birch. Some bogs lack even these plants and consist entirely of herbaceous low-growing species such as Bog Cranberry, Marsh Cottongrass, Pitcher Plant and a wide variety of mosses.

Bogs appear to have been created by a combination of irregular drainage and highly acidic water. Plant growth is limited by these conditions to specially adapted species.

Birds found in the open spruce bogs include:

Spruce Grouse (nests)　　　　Palm Warbler (uncommon)
Yellow-bellied Flycatcher　　Connecticut Warbler
Ruby-crowned Kinglet　　　　Le Conte's Sparrow
　(edges in larger trees)　　　(occasional)
Hermit Thrush　　　　　　　Lincoln's Sparrow
Tennessee Warbler　　　　　Swamp Sparrow
Nashville Warbler　　　　　　Dark-eyed Junco

In many bogs the Black Spruce will gradually increase in size and density attracting additional birds characteristic of the coniferous forest.

<u>Open Black Spruce Bog Habitat</u>

# Upland Coniferous Forest

The coniferous forests of the north predominate the landscape. The upland coniferous forest consists mainly of Jack Pine, Balsam Fir, White Spruce, and to a lesser degree, White Pine and Red Pine. Some stands may be pure in composition and large areas may be covered by a single species such as Jack Pine. In most instances, due to topography and soil conditions, a mix of coniferous species prevails. This variety results in habitat attractive to a large number of bird species. These include:

Sharp-shinned Hawk
Northern Goshawk
   (uncommon)
Broad-winged Hawk
Merlin
Spruce Grouse
Barred Owl
Eastern Wood-Pewee
Gray Jay
Common Raven
Black-capped Chickadee
Boreal Chickadee
Red-breasted Nuthatch
Brown Creeper
Golden-crowned Kinglet
Ruby-crowned Kinglet

Swainson's Thrush
Hermit Thrush
Solitary Vireo
Nashville Warbler
Magnolia Warbler
Cape May Warbler
Yellow-rumped Warbler
Pine Warbler
Bay-breasted Warbler
   (uncommon)
Ovenbird
Canada Warbler
Red Crossbill
   (irregular)
Pine Siskin
Evening Grosbeak

Upland Coniferous Forest Habitat

# Lowland Coniferous Forest

This habitat consists of dense stands of Black Spruce occasionally interspersed with Tamarack, Balsam Fir and Jack Pine. Because the dominant trees create a total shade condition on the forest floor, secondary vegetation levels may be almost non-existent, with shrubs limited to Labrador Tea and alder. Many pure Black Spruce stands have an attractive and interesting array of mosses covering the ground beneath the trees. The Black Spruce forest is a unique feature of the boreal forest and the cool shaded conditions are attractive to a number of bird specimens typical of the north.

Lowland coniferous species include:

| | |
|---|---|
| Spruce Grouse | Hermit Thrush |
| Black-backed Woodpecker | Solitary Vireo |
| Olive-sided Flycatcher | Nashville Warbler |
| Gray Jay | Magnolia Warbler |
| Boreal Chickadee | Yellow-rumped Warbler |
| Red-breasted Nuthatch | Black-throated Green Warbler |
| Winter Wren | Northern Waterthrush |
| Golden-crowned Kinglet | Chipping Sparrow |
| Ruby-crowned Kinglet | Pine Siskin |
| Swainson's Thrush | Evening Grosbeak |

Lowland Coniferous Forest Habitat

# Cattail-Bulrush Marsh

Unfortunately, this particular habitat is not at all common in Quetico. It is limited to a few small sites scattered throughout the park. Outside Quetico, near the Town of Atikokan, there are several large cattail marshes that provide exciting birding. The largest marsh is located in Steep Rock Lake. It was created as a result of water level changes made during the initial development of the now defunct Steep Rock Iron Mine. The extensive stands of cattail and bulrush in Steep Rock Lake have an excitement and character that only marshes possess. Birding in them can be extremely rewarding. Other cattail marsh areas near Atikokan include the Lower Basin "A" area, the Auxiliary Rawn Reservoirs and the southeast arm of the former Steep Rock Lake.

The mouth of the Atikokan river is another noteworthy marsh. It contains extensive stands of cattail, bulrush, reed grass and Wild Rice. In addition there is an extensive grass marsh near Caribus Creek with its attendant bird population.

The large marshes of the Atikokan area have a decidedly western flavour as indicated by the following list of birds to be found in them:

| | |
|---|---|
| Pied-billed Grebe | Common Snipe |
| Red-necked Grebe (rare) | Wilson's Phalarope |
| American Bittern | (migrant) |
| Great Blue Heron | Black Tern |
| Wood Duck | Alder Flycatcher |
| American Black Duck | (marsh edges) |

| | |
|---|---|
| Mallard | Sedge Wren |
| Blue-winged Teal | Common Yellowthroat |
| American Widgeon | Le Conte's Sparrow |
| Ring-necked Duck | Song Sparrow |
| Osprey | Swamp Sparrow |
| Bald Eagle | Red-winged Blackbird |
| Northern Harrier | Yellow-headed Blackbird |
| Virginia Rail (rare) | Common Grackle |
| Sora | |
| American Coot | |

During the spring migration, the marshes are often the first areas to be free of ice and, as a result, large flocks of waterfowl of many species concentrate on the patches of open water.

Cattail Marsh Habitat

<u>Grassy Marsh Habitat</u>

# Deciduous Forest

Deciduous forest is another major component of the northern boreal forest and is characterized by Trembling Aspen and White Birch with lesser amounts of Balsam Poplar and Red Maple scattered throughout. In most sites, a scattering of conifer is also present, often as an understorey. The understorey is usually quite dense as the somewhat open nature of the canopy allows sunlight to reach the forest floor. Hazel, Mountain Maple, dogwood and a profusion of herbaceous species form a thick growth of mixed vegetation. In most cases, the deciduous forest is temporary; the first stage in the successional path to a predominantly coniferous climax forest.

Because of the variation in the age and composition of the deciduous forest, a large number of birds are found therein and include:

| | |
|---|---|
| Broad-winged Hawk | Black-throated Blue |
| Ruffed Grouse | Warbler (rare) |
| Yellow-bellied | Black-and-white |
| Sapsucker | Warbler |
| Downy Woodpecker | American Redstart |
| Hairy Woodpecker | Ovenbird |
| Pileated Woodpecker | Mourning Warbler |
| Least Flycatcher | Canada Warbler |
| Blue Jay | Scarlet Tanager |
| Philadelphia Vireo | Rose-breasted Grosbeak |
| (uncommon) | White-throated Sparrow |
| Red-eyed Vireo | Purple Finch |
| Northern Parula | |
| Magnolia Warbler | |

Deciduous Forest Habitat

# Urban - The Town of Atikokan

Bisected by the Atikokan River, the Town of Atikokan is a significant bird habitat. Many species that are scarce or of infrequent occurrence elsewhere in the forested parts of the area can be observed in town.

The Atikokan River winds slowly through the town. The bushy banks and wooded floodplain interspersed with open lawns and clearings make it a must for the birder. A morning float trip by canoe from one end of town to the other in early June will ensure the birder of at least 50 species of birds.

Winter birding in the Atikokan area can be rather unproductive. A day spent in the bush in February may result in a total list of only 10 species. In town, however, this total could be doubled, no doubt due to the large numbers of feeders that are maintained by interested people. Christmas bird counts, carried out in the town since 1960, have recorded a total of 50 species with an average of 18 species for each count.

The following species can be observed in Atikokan:

| | |
|---|---|
| Killdeer | Veery |
| Common Snipe | American Robin |
| Woodcock | Gray Catbird |
| Mourning Dove | Brown Thrasher |
| (uncommon) | Cedar Waxwing |
| Black-billed Cuckoo | Red-eyed Vireo |
| Common Nighthawk | Yellow Warbler |
| Chimney Swift | Chestnut-sided Warbler |

Ruby-throated
   Hummingbird
Eastern Kingbird
Tree Swallow
Bank Swallow
Cliff Swallow
   (abundant)
Barn Swallow
American Crow
Common Raven
House Wren

Indigo Bunting
Savannah Sparrow
Song Sparrow
Brewer's Blackbird
Purple Finch
Common Redpoll
American Goldfinch
Evening Grosbeak

Residential Atikokan and the Atikokan River

## Seasons and Birds

Winter begins to loosen its grip on the land in Quetico in mid-March. The very first of the migrants - American Crows, Bald Eagles and waterfowl - make their welcome appearance. As the snow melts and the lakes clear of ice, there is a rush of arriving birds which peaks about the middle of May. Quetico is noted for its breeding warblers. On a single day, an observer may record more than 20 species that are on their breeding territories, in full song.

Once breeding has finished in late July the forests of Quetico fall silent, and while birds are abundant, they are not in song and become difficult to find. The first fall migrants are shorebirds that usually appear in late July and early August. The first week in September produces a major movement of warblers and by early October, sparrows seem to fill the woods. The last of the waterfowl have left by early November. By early December the first winter snows are once again covering the land.

With the exception of ever-present Gray Jays and Common Ravens, few birds are found in Quetico during the winter. The deep silences are only occasionally broken by the calls of Boreal Chickadees or the light tapping of a woodpecker.

In Atikokan, many people put food out for birds in the winter and large flocks of Evening and Pine Grosbeaks are attracted. Common Redpolls and Purple Finches remain in large numbers some winters and may be totally absent the next.

Quetico in winter is a silent place, the solitude broken only by an occasional croak from a Common Raven flying overhead.

# Relative Abundance and Seasonal Occurrence

The designation of "relative abundance" of birds in Quetico and the Atikokan area is of course purely subjective. The following classifications will at least provide the birder in the area with some indication of the probability of seeing a particular species.

"Seasonal occurrence" is somewhat more exacting than "relative abundance" and is also provided to assist birders visiting or planning to visit the area.

## Relative Abundance

Common: easily found in suitable habitat at appropriate time of year - e.g. White-throated Sparrow, Red-eyed Vireo.

Frequent: less easily found in suitable habitat but several can be encountered in a day with a little effort in suitable habitat - e.g. Pied-billed Grebe, Mourning Warbler.

Uncommon: to be found each day in small numbers in suitable habitat with a good effort. May be restricted to a specific habitat or location - e.g. Gray Catbird, Wilson's Warbler.

Occasional: found in small numbers each year (one to five records) but may be erratic and unpredictable regarding time of year and habitat preference - e.g. Western

Meadowlark, Bohemian Waxwing.

Rare: not recorded every year but to be expected - e.g. Virginia Rail, Boreal Owl.

Vagrant: not to be expected, usually only one or two records in total for area - e.g. Varied Thrush, Prothonotary Warbler.

## Seasonal Occurrence

Permanent Resident: breeds and is present in the area throughout the year in suitable habitat.

Summer Resident: breeds and is present in the area during the breeding season in suitable habitat.

Summer Visitor: visits the area during the breeding season but does not breed.

Winter Visitor: visits the area during the non-breeding season.

Transient: passes through the area during spring and fall migration.

# SPECIES ACCOUNTS

# Common Loon

*Gavia immer*

Common - Summer Resident

  The Common Loon is a prominent feature of Quetico. It is undoubtedly observed and heard by every canoeist travelling in the park. Loons arrive in the park as soon as the first patches of open water occur in the winter's ice. This may be as early as the second week in April or as late as the first week in May. Every suitably-sized lake appears to have at least one breeding pair of loons. During the summer, concentrations of apparent non-breeding birds occur on some of the larger lakes in the park, most notably on Bailey Bay of Basswood Lake. This group of birds, present every year, may include 125 individuals and is a delight to canoeists who may suddenly find themselves surrounded by loons. The last loons leave the park and the Atikokan area usually by the third week in November when the larger lakes freeze.

Earliest date: April 17
Latest date: November 27

Gisela © '93

## Common Loon

# Pied-billed Grebe

*Podilymbus podiceps*

Common - Summer Resident

Found throughout the park and the Atikokan area, in all areas with suitable habitat, the Pied-billed Grebe is more common than most park visitors realize. Its secretive nature and the fact that most canoe routes bypass the marshy areas it frequents account for its apparent scarcity. During migration it may be seen almost anywhere, particularly in the spring, when it arrives soon after the first small openings in the ice appear. When breeding, it stays in the marshes and the only indication of its presence is its call. In the large marshes of Steep Rock Lake and Apungsisagin Lake, numbers of this grebe nest. Quiet paddling through the cattails and bulrushes is frequently rewarded by the sight of a mother grebe quickly covering her eggs with sodden water plants as she slips off the small mound of floating vegetation that serves as a nest.

Earliest date:  March 28
Latest date:  October 14

# Horned Grebe

*Podiceps auritus*

Occasional - Summer Resident

Uncommon - Transient

This grebe is present in the park and the Atikokan area only during the spring and fall migration periods. At times surprisingly large concentrations of migrating grebes are encountered. Several flocks of 50 or more birds have been recorded spring and fall on Batchewaung, Pickerel and Clearwater West Lakes.

Lack of suitable habitat in Quetico has resulted in an absence of breeding. Outside the park, one record of breeding (a family consisting of flightless young and two adults) on Marmion Lake is unique.

Earliest date: April 14
Latest date: December 23

# Red-necked Grebe

*Podiceps grisegena*

Occasional - Summer Resident

Uncommon - Transient

The Red-necked Grebe is an uncommon spring and fall migrant on the larger lakes in the park and the Atikokan area. Spring records are few; the birds migrate through very quickly unless stopped by inclement weather. Fall migration is more prolonged, most birds being noted again on the larger lakes. This grebe has not been recorded as breeding in Quetico. Cattail and bulrush marshes in the park are small and infrequent, which likely accounts for the lack of breeding.

On Steep Rock Lake north of Quetico large stands of cattails and bulrushes provide suitable habitat and one or two pairs of grebes nest occasionally.

Earliest date: April 26
Latest date:  October 11


# Western Grebe
*Aechmophorus occidentalis*

Vagrant

The largest and most impressive of the grebes, the Western Grebe has been recorded once in the area. It should be watched for on the larger lakes of the park in spring and early fall. On August 28, 1978, Walshe observed two Western Grebes on Lac la Croix.


# American White Pelican
*Pelecanus erythrorhynchos*

Vagrant

One record of this spectacular bird exists for

Quetico. On June 6, 1977, one was observed flying over Lac la Croix. An additional record just north of Atikokan consists of a single bird present for several days on a small lake. It was first noted on September 16, 1964. A thriving population of White Pelicans is located on a group of islands in the south end of Lake of the Woods. The huge birds are a common sight in that area, some 240 km. west of Quetico. The Lake of the Woods colony is one of the most easterly breeding locations of this western species. On June 6, 1991, a flock of 35 was noted near Finlayson Lake, just north of Atikokan and 3 were present on Finlayson Lake, June 29, 1991.

## Double-crested Cormorant
*Phalacrocorax auritus*

Occasional - Transient

This species appears in the park and the Atikokan area on an intermittent basis, usually during migration. A common breeding bird of the large lakes to the west, (Rainy Lake and Lake of the Woods), it appears to be increasing. Gull colonies on the larger park lakes should be carefully scanned as cormorant nesting is a distinct possibility in the future as the species expands its range.

Earliest date: May 5
Latest date: October 29

## American Bittern

*Botaurus lentiginosus*

Frequent - Summer Resident

Bitterns are most easily located in the spring by their strange calls. Reed and grass marshes, open bogs and swampy lakeshores are preferred habitats. The birds are difficult to see because of their secretive nature and a plumage that blends perfectly with their surroundings. They are most frequently seen when canoeists flush them from the edges of marshy streams. The bittern leaves with a squawk and a flap of wings, and when this happens almost beside the canoe, it is debatable who is the most startled -- the bird or the canoeist.

Bitterns nest on the ground in wet areas and discovery of the nest is usually accidental. A female bittern defending her eggs or newly-hatched young is an impressive sight as she fluffs out her feathers and growls menacingly. If the intruder approaches closely enough she lashes out with her sharp bill.

Earliest date:  April 25
Latest date:  September 24

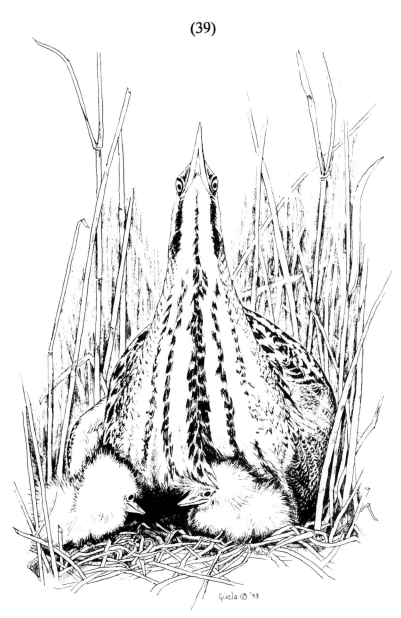

**American Bittern**

# Least Bittern

*Ixobrychus exilis*

Rare - Summer Resident

On August 21, 1984, a Least Bittern was found in downtown Atikokan. The bird was an immature, with tufts of down adhering to its feathers. The bird was uninjured and after being kept for 3 days it was released in a nearby cattail marsh, apparently in good health.

The record was the first for the Atikokan area and the Rainy River District.


# Great Blue Heron

*Ardea herodias*

Common - Summer Resident

Great Blue Herons arrive in the park and the Atikokan area several weeks before the lakes are ice-free. They congregate along small streams wherever there is open water. As spring advances, the birds spread out and return to the numerous nesting colonies throughout the area. Most nesting sites are in stands of conifers, frequently on islands or peninsulas. One colony on Basswood Lake is in a stand of mature Red Pine and the nests are over 80 feet from the ground. The birds are very faithful to the nesting site and many colonies have been in existence for years. After the young leave the nest, herons can be seen almost anywhere. Immature birds can be sometimes closely approached by canoe as they stand silently on a lakeshore.

Herons leave the area rather early in the fall. It is unusual to see any after the middle of October.

Earliest date: March 19
Latest date: October 12

## Great Egret
*Casmerodius albus*

Vagrant

On August 9, 1992, a Great Egret arrived at Finlayson Resort on Finlayson Lake, 16 km. north of Atikokan. It stayed until August 20 and was the first record for the area.

## Tundra Swan
*Cygnus columbianus*

Occasional - Transient

With one exception, all records are for the spring. The park is apparently east of the major flyway used by swans on their way to and from their arctic breeding grounds. As a result, district records likely involve small flocks and individuals that have strayed from the main flight lines. When the birds do visit the area they tend to stay for several days, apparently resting, before continuing their migration.

Earliest date:  May 11
Latest date:  November 9

## Snow Goose

*Chen caerulescens*

Frequent - Transient

Snow Geese pass through the area each spring and fall.  The autumn flights are heavier since the flocks include the young of the year. Weather plays an important part in the migration of this species. Good weather permits the flocks to fly right over without stopping and migration may be over in a very few days if favourable conditions persist.

In most years, however, a few flocks or individuals are forced to land and, being grazers, are attracted to open grassy areas.  In the falls of 1980 and 1993 it was quite common to see small groups of Snow Geese walking about the school grounds and Legion Point in Atikokan, quite unconcerned with their urban surroundings.

Earliest date:  April 23
Latest date:  October 16

# Canada Goose

*Branta canadensis*

Common - Transient

Flocks of Canada Geese cross the park and the Atikokan area each spring and fall. Good weather conditions allow the flocks to pass over without landing, and on good days flights are heavy. The Canada Goose apparently does not breed in the park as summer records are few. Ducks Unlimited introduced Canada Geese to the Atikokan area in 1985 when about 80 flightless young were released near the Ontario Hydro Generating Station. In 1987 at least one pair raised young on Finlayson Lake, a few miles west of the original release site and since then, a few pairs breed in the area each year.

Earliest date: March 28
Latest date: November 10

# Wood Duck

*Aix sponsa*

Uncommon - Summer Resident

This beautiful duck appears to be at the edge of its range in the Quetico area. Although Wood Ducks appear with other migrating waterfowl early in the spring, they are among the first to leave in the fall. Most are gone by the third week in September.

Wood Ducks are noted throughout the breeding season but no indication of nesting has been recorded. A number of nesting boxes suitable for the species have been erected throughout the Atikokan area but so far only Common Goldeneyes and Hooded Mergansers have made use of them.

The Wood Duck frequents the smaller ponds and streams in the area. It has a decided preference for beaver ponds with many standing dead trees.

Earliest date:  April 9
Latest date:  October 14

## Green-winged Teal

*Anas crecca*

Common - Transient

Occasional - Summer Resident

Another member of the large flocks of migrating waterfowl that collect in the patches of open water in the spring, most Green-winged Teal continue northward and westward to breed.

The drake is a beautiful little bird but is by no means timid. Arriving already paired, the drakes take exception to anyone paying even the slightest bit of attention to their mates.  A sudden rush with splashing wings, outstretched neck and open bill quickly repel any other drake brash enough to show interest in another drake's mate.

This species appears to favour smaller ponds and streams with abundant marshy shorelines for breeding sites. The two area breeding records, one of recently-hatched young, and one of a nest with eggs, were made in such sites.

Earliest date:  April 13
Latest date:  September 27


## American Black Duck
*Anas rubripes*

Common - Summer Resident

Similar to the Mallard in its catholic habitat requirements and habits, it is perhaps a little less common, nearing the western extremity of its range.  This duck favours small ponds and areas flooded by beaver activity. Sometimes it is quite happy to pass the summer on a surprisingly small body of water.

One nest found in the park was hidden under a small juniper bush right on the edge of a 50-foot lakeside cliff.  On leaving the nest, the duck simply launched itself over the edge of the cliff and was away.  While ducks may not have an appreciation of their surroundings, the view from this particular nest was quite spectacular.

Earliest date:  April 1
Latest date:  December 24

# Mallard

*Anas platyrhynchos*

Common - Summer Resident

The Mallard is one of the common breeding ducks of the park and the Atikokan area. Another early spring migrant, the flights of several drakes in pursuit of a single duck are frequently observed as pairing is finalized. Some birds appear to arrive already paired.

The Mallard places its nest almost anywhere on the ground. Usually it is sheltered by a small bush or shrub. The duck sits closely and explodes off the down-lined nest at the last moment.

This duck has infrequently remained in the area through the winter. Sections of streams kept open by a strong current and supporting an adequate food supply are apparently all the bird needs to survive, even at temperatures of -40 deg. C.

Earliest date: March 8
Latest date: December 24

# Northern Pintail

*Anas acuta*

Uncommon - Transient

This duck does not appear to stay in the area after the spring migration. Fall records are few and hunters in the area only occasionally shoot Northern Pintails.

The impressively-plumaged drakes and their slim brown mates are seen in the early spring in the company of other migrating waterfowl. Frequenting by necessity the small patches of open water available at that time, flocks of up to 20 birds or more are sometimes observed. They appear to stay in the area only until open water is available further north.

A flock of flying young observed on Marmion Lake in late August of 1975 suggests possible local breeding but this needs confirmation.

Earliest date:  April 11
Latest date:  October 6

## Blue-winged Teal

*Anas discors*

Common - Transient

Frequent - Summer Resident

This small waterfowl is one of the last to arrive in the spring and the first to depart in the fall.  It is not inclined to endure cold water.

Breeding occurs in marshy areas that have abundant emergent vegetation in which the young find both food and shelter.  In common with other members of the duck family, nests are quite often located at some distance from water. The mother leads her new brood to water as soon as they are capable of leaving the nest site.

The Blue-winged Teal is frequently noted by canoeists along marshy, slow-moving streams and can usually be quite closely approached.

Earliest date:  March 31
Latest date:  September 27


## Northern Shoveler
*Anas clypeata*

Occasional - Transient

This species is recorded every year in the area during the spring migration but in very few numbers. To see half a dozen in total in spring is exceptional. No fall records have been made.

Although no records of breeding exist, a pair seen in June of 1973 suggest the occasional pair may nest. These birds were noted in the large cattail marshes of Steep Rock Lake, a habitat not unlike the favoured western sloughs.

Earliest date:  April 22
Latest date:  October 2

# Gadwall
*Anas strepera*

Vagrant

This species has been occasionally reported by hunters. Confirmation of the species' presence occurred on September 28, 1988 when the author was shown an immature bird taken by a hunter. On April 18, 1992, a pair were noted on a small patch of open water on Moose Lake.

# American Wigeon
*Anas americana*

Frequent - Transient

The Baldpate, as it is also known, joins the spring flocks of migrating waterfowl that remain in the area only until open water is available further north. There are no records of breeding in the area but birds of the year are sometimes taken by hunters early in the season (mid-September). This, together with an occasional adult being noted during the summer, would indicate probable nesting.

Earliest date: April 15
Latest date: September 21

# Canvasback

*Aythya valisineria*

Rare - Transient

Similar to the Redhead, this impressive duck is only a rare visitor to the area. The large spring flocks of migrating waterfowl should be carefully looked over for this species. There are no fall records.

Earliest date:  April 29
Latest date:  May 4

# Redhead

*Aythya americana*

Rare - Transient

This diving duck should be looked for in the big mixed flocks of migrating waterfowl in the spring. There is only one record for Quetico, made on Pickerel Lake, May 10, 1985.

Earliest date:  April 16
Latest date:  November 2

# Ring-necked Duck

*Aythya collaris*

Common - Summer Resident

After arrival in the spring, pairs of Ring-necked Ducks scatter throughout the district and breed on the smaller ponds and weedy sheltered bogs on larger lakes. Nests with eggs have been found in the Steep Rock Lake marshes. Several broods of recently-hatched young have been noted elsewhere. Toward the end of summer it is not uncommon to encounter flocks of young and old Ring-necked Ducks totalling 200 or more individuals.

Earliest date: April 11
Latest date: November 27

# Greater Scaup

*Aythya marila*

Occasional - Transient

Confusion with the Lesser Scaup likely accounts for the scarcity of records for this species. It occurs each spring in small numbers and can usually be encountered at a few particular locations such as at French Lake in the northeast corner of Quetico. There is only one fall record, that of an injured bird rescued from the Steep Rock Iron Mine open pit.

Earliest date: April 16
Latest date: November 19

# Lesser Scaup
*Aythya affinis*

Frequent - Transient

The most frequently-observed migrant diving duck, the Lesser Scaup passes through the park and the Atikokan area in large numbers, spring and fall. The last birds leave just before the larger lakes freeze over in late November.

In the spring the flocks contain a significantly higher proportion of drakes. As a result, the females are the subject of constant attention by a number of males. The flocks are in a state of constant motion both on the water and in the air. There is no indication the species breeds in the area.

Earliest date:  March 20
Latest date:  November 22


# Harlequin Duck
*Histrionicus histrionicus*

Vagrant

This visitor from the west has been recorded only twice in the area. Peruniak observed 2 males and a female on Upper Basin "A" near the Caland Mine on May 16, 1963. An immature male was with a flock of Common Goldeneyes March 29, 1989 at the Finlayson Lake Diversion.

## Oldsquaw
*Clangula hyemalis*

Vagrant

A single flock of Oldsquaw was noted on Saganagons Lake in the southeast corner of Quetico on May 21, 1974. This species should be watched for during the spring and fall migration periods.

## Black Scoter
*Melanitta nigra*

Vagrant

On September 29, 1963, two Black Scoters were observed on Nym Lake. The second area record, over 10 years later, consisted of two birds that remained on French Lake in Quetico Park from October 1 to October 18, 1974.

## White-winged Scoter
*Melanitta fusca*

Rare - Transient

The few spring records for this duck indicate the Atikokan area is not within its main migration route. Most records have been from the larger lakes such as Marmion

Lake, immediately after breakup.  It should be looked for. There are no fall records.

Earliest date:  May 11
Latest date:  May 24

# Common Goldeneye

*Bucephala clangula*

Common - Summer Resident

Frequent - Permanent Resident

The goldeneye is the common breeding diving duck of the area. Females, sometimes accompanied by males, are frequently seen flying through stands of large trees in the spring looking for suitable nesting sites.  Former nesting cavities of the Pileated Woodpecker are favoured. The species has used boxes placed in trees for arboreal nesting ducks.  When encountered by canoeists, female goldeneyes put on an impressive distraction display to draw attention from their attractively marked ducklings.  The young dive readily and can remain underwater a surprising length of time. This species appears to finalize pairing shortly after arriving in the spring.

Common Goldeneyes winter regularly in the area, most particularly on the fast-flowing water of the Finlayson Lake Diversion.  The birds are quite unaffected by temperatures as low as -45 deg. C. as they go about the business of diving for food.

# Bufflehead

*Bucephala albeola*

Uncommon - Transient

The tiny Bufflehead is a regular but uncommon visitor to the Atikokan area each spring and fall. It is one of the last of the waterfowl to leave the area in the fall and may be present on the larger lakes until late November. Rarely are more than half a dozen seen together; usually only single birds or pairs are encountered.

Earliest date: April 14
Latest date: November 16

# Hooded Merganser

*Lophodytes cucullatus*

Common - Summer Resident

Found throughout the area, this small fish-eating duck frequents small beaver ponds, marshy creeks and weedy bays of the larger lakes during the breeding season. The Hooded Merganser nests in holes in trees and, like the Common Goldeneye, can be seen flying through the lakeshore forests in the spring searching for a suitable nest cavity.

It is a hardy species and remains in the area in fall until the lakes freeze completely over.

It is commonly seen by canoeists on small winding marshy creeks and can usually be closely approached.

Earliest date:  March 28
Latest date:  December 19

**Hooded Merganser**

# Common Merganser

*Mergus merganser*

Common - Summer Resident

As its name implies, this merganser is very common in Quetico. It is the duck most often seen by canoeists who encounter the large black and white males with brilliant red bills in the spring, the brown-crested female with downy young in the early summer and large flocks of fully grown young in the latter part of the summer. When surprised, flightless young in turn surprise the canoeist as they put on an amazing burst of speed and literally run across the water in an effort to escape. The Common Merganser nests in a variety of locations; under buildings, in hollow logs or stumps, in nest boxes or holes in trees large enough to admit the female, and in nooks and crannies under shoreline boulders. They are quite faithful to the nesting site and return year after year.

This duck is one of the earliest spring arrivals, seeking out tiny patches of open water in rapids or creek mouths long before the lakes and ponds are ice-free. One winter record exists; that of a female-plumaged bird observed January 1, 1987 in the open water between Icy and Snow lakes.

Earliest date:  March 28
Latest date:  January 1

# Red-breasted Merganser

*Mergus serrator*

Uncommon - Transient

This merganser passes through the park and the Atikokan area with the spring flocks of migrating waterfowl. Their numbers are usually quite small but if there is a slow-down in the spring breakup, flocks of several dozen birds can build up. It is another species that spends little time in the area, moving through as quickly as weather conditions permit. There are a few summer records with pairs noted on Finlayson, Clearwater West and White Otter lakes and it is possible the species breeds in the area.

Earliest date: April 24
Latest date: November 15

# Turkey Vulture

*Cathartes aura*

Frequent - Summer Resident

The clear days of midsummer with their scattered white puffy clouds are a canoeist's delight. Passing by rocky cliffs that drop straight into the water, large dark birds are often noted floating overhead with hardly a wingbeat. Although most canoeists usually do not know what they are, the birds are Turkey Vultures. Fairly common throughout the park, vultures are usually seen flying. In company with Common Ravens and the occasional Bald Eagle, they are sometimes encountered on a beach or a shoreline boulder eating the remains of fish caught by anglers.

The Turkey Vulture breeds in the area, utilizing the small cave-like spaces in the jumbled rocks of cliff-base talus slopes. Flightless young have been noted on shoreline talus slopes on Nym Lake and Namakan Lake.

Outside Quetico, the best place to consistently see Turkey Vultures is at any of the small landfill sites found throughout the Atikokan area. It is sometimes possible to see ten to fifteen of the birds perched in the trees surrounding such a landfill site.

Earliest date: April 2
Latest date: November 3


## Osprey

*Pandion haliaetus*

Uncommon - Summer Resident

The Osprey is found in small numbers throughout the park and the Atikokan area. Pairs arrive in the spring shortly after the ice leaves the larger lakes (and fish, their chief food, becomes available) and return to their traditional nesting sites. Osprey nests are large stick structures that are nearly always placed at the top of a broken-off dead tree. The tree may be on the shoreline of a lake or standing in water but easy, unhindered access for the birds and a commanding view are two consistent site requirements. The nests are usually high but one on Marmion Lake, on a large broken tree surrounded by water, is only a few feet above the surface.

Canoeists are often surprised to see this light-coloured, long-winged hawk plunge completely below the surface, leaving a moment later with a fish firmly held in its large talons. One or two flaps of the wings are followed by a burst of spray as the bird rids its plumage of water.

Earliest date:  April 17
Latest date:  October 6

## Bald Eagle

*Haliaeetus leucocephalus*

Frequent - Summer Resident

Rare - Winter Visitor

Quetico is Bald Eagle country. The large number of lakes in the park and the rest of the Atikokan area support a significant population of this endangered species. A total of 50 nest sites have been located, 30 in Quetico and 20 in the rest of the area. Nests are usually placed in large White Pines, well down from the top of the tree. The nest, even though very large, can be quite difficult to see as it blends well with the clumpy foliage pattern of the White Pine.

Bald Eagles appear to have increased in numbers in the past few years, perhaps as a result of the reduction in pesticide and herbicide use. One nest on Mackenzie Lake fledged 3 young in 1979, an unusual occurrence.

Bald Eagles return to their territories in early March. A nest site on French Lake has been watched for many years and the annual spring arrival of the adults can usually be predicted within a few days. A scattering of records indicate some eagles may stay throughout the winter. These are likely birds from more northerly locations that found an adequate food supply (open water) in the area to carry them through the winter. The Bald Eagle and the Common Loon are two park birds that most visitors will see and remember as part of their wilderness experience.

Earliest date: February 28
Latest date: January 11


## Northern Harrier

*Circus cyaneus*

Frequent - Transient

Uncommon - Resident

This interesting hawk is most frequently observed during the spring and fall migration periods. A few pairs stay in the area to nest, utilizing open marshy or boggy

**<u>Bald Eagle</u>**

patches that are usually found along slow-moving streams. A typical nesting site is located at the mouth of the Atikokan River. Here an open grassy marsh sprinkled with clumps of willow and Leatherleaf annually attract a pair of Northern Harriers. The nest is placed on the ground, surrounded by dense vegetation, but open above for easy access.

The spectacular flight display of the silvery-gray male, although seldom observed, is a sure indication that a pair has established a breeding territory.

Earliest date: April 9
Latest date: September 19

## Sharp-shinned Hawk

*Accipiter striatus*

Uncommon - Summer Resident

Frequent - Transient

Most frequently noted during migration, especially in early September, this small accipiter is an efficient predator of small birds. Occasionally Sharp-shinned Hawks are noted high over the treetops soaring on outspread wings and tail or moving along very deliberately with a flap and glide flight. Most often the view of this hawk is a fleeting glimpse as it adeptly flickers through the forest, quite near the ground.

The very few breeding records reflect the observers' inability to investigate vast areas of forest rather than the scarcity of the species.

Earliest date:   April 6
Latest date:   October 7

# Cooper's Hawk

*Accipiter cooperii*

Occasional - Transient

The scarcity of records for this bird may be in part caused by the difficulty in separating it from the other two species of accipiters. Nonetheless, it appears to be at best an occasional visitor to the area.

Earliest date:   May 4
Latest date:   September 18

# Northern Goshawk

*Accipiter gentilis*

Rare - Permanent Resident

Occasional - Transient and Winter Resident

The status of the Northern Goshawk in the area is far from clear.  Most birds are observed during the spring and fall migration as they move through the area.  There are several breeding records and it is likely that it is more common than realized due to the vast inaccessible wooded areas of the park, and the somewhat secretive nature of this hawk. Certainly the migration periods are the best times to look for the bird.

Northern Goshawks have been recorded during all the winter months. The winter birds are likely individuals that have moved in from much farther north. A fierce and efficient predator of grouse and Snowshoe Hare, signs left in the snow once showed where one had attacked a hare, followed it on foot into a thick alder tangle, and succeeded in catching the unfortunate creature.

## Red-shouldered Hawk
*Buteo lineatus*

Vagrant

The one apparent record for the park was made on June 10, 1971, on the upper part of the Cache River. There has been none since. This hawk should be looked for, especially in the spring.

## Broad-winged Hawk
*Buteo platypterus*

Common - Summer Resident

This medium-sized buteo is found throughout the park and the Atikokan area. The hawks arrive shortly after the last of the snow is gone in the spring and draw

**Northern Goshawk**

attention to their arrival by their whistling calls. Broad-winged Hawks feed, at least in the spring, to a large degree on frogs and can often be seen sitting on roadside trees and telephone wires intently watching small pools of water for prey.

Broad-wings nest in both conifer and deciduous trees but have a definite preference for Trembling Aspen. Some nests are used for several years in succession, apparently by the same pair of birds.

The hawks are seldom seen after mid-September, leaving the area shortly after the first frosts occur. The large migrating flocks observed in the more southerly parts of the range are not found here; the birds just quietly slip away.

Earliest date:  April 14
Latest date:  September 22

## Swainson's Hawk
*Buteo swainsoni*

Vagrant

There are two records for this western hawk; one in Quetico Park at French Lake on June 28, 1968, and on May 7, 1993 in Atikokan. The Atikokan bird was a light phase individual. The proximity of the park to Manitoba and points west increases the chance of this hawk being observed in the area and it should be watched for.

# Red-tailed Hawk

*Buteo jamaicensis*

Uncommon - Summer Resident

The vast unbroken forests of Quetico are not good habitat for this hawk. The best places to look for it are out of the park in the large areas that have been logged. Here it finds the open spaces for hunting and scattered groups of large trees suitable for nesting that it prefers.

There is a noticeable increase in these hawks during the fall and several may be noted during a day of travel through the logged areas of the district.

Earliest date:  March 26
Latest date:  October 29


# Rough-legged Hawk

*Buteo lagopus*

Occasional - Transient

This impressive hawk is present in the area only during the spring and fall migration periods.  The continuous forests of Quetico do not provide the open habitat favoured by this buteo, and park records are usually of birds soaring high overhead.

Occasionally, birds perched in marshes or other small openings are encountered.  The open cutover areas out of the park attract the migrating hawks and are the best places to watch for them. Although birds with light-phase plumages predominate, dark-phased individuals and some with interesting intermediate plumage are regularly recorded. Numbers do not seem to vary significantly between spring and fall. The general over-all abundance of Rough-legged Hawks is relative to annual breeding success, food availability and wintering success. All of these factors affect park records.

Earliest date: April 2
Latest date: November 20

## Golden Eagle
*Aquila chrysaetos*

Vagrant

There are four records for this magnificent bird. The first, in Quetico Park, was of an individual that was accidentally caught in a trap at French Lake in the winter of 1936. The second record was of an immature bird seen in a cutover on November 18, 1981. The third, a superb adult, was caught in a trap on October 28, 1983 and released unharmed. The fourth bird, an adult, was observed near Snow Lake April 16, 1990. Golden Eagles likely pass through the area each spring and fall in very small numbers. It is difficult to separate immature Bald Eagles and Golden Eagles and this may account for the lack of additional records.

Golden Eagles generally prefer more open habitat, not provided in the forests of Quetico.

# American Kestrel

*Falco sparverius*

Frequent - Summer Resident

Not a bird of the mature forest, the Kestrel has benefited from the large open areas created by logging activity, hydro line corridors and highways. It will also move into burns and remain as a breeding bird until the forest growth is too dense for it to obtain the small mammal and insect prey it depends on. The Kestrel is not easily found in Quetico due to the lack of suitable open areas. However, in the large cutovers outside the park it is fairly common. Several pairs nest in the town of Atikokan, utilizing old woodpecker holes or nesting boxes placed for their use in trees.

The first Kestrels arrive in the spring before all the snow has melted. They can easily be seen as they sit on roadside utility wires and scan the snow-free highway edges for prey. After nesting, the family groups slowly disperse southward and late fall records are uncommon.

Earliest date: April 2
Latest date: September 26

Gisela © '93

**American Kestrel**

# Merlin

*Falco columbarius*

Uncommon - Summer Resident

Quetico is an excellent place to see this small falcon - another of the birds of prey that have suffered significant population declines as a result of pesticide residues. The Merlin seems to favour small pine-clad islands for breeding sites and frequently returns to the same site year after year.

They noisily defend their island, and canoeists who happen to pass by will be scolded until well beyond the bird's territory. Constant calling and circular flights on rapidly quivering wings are sure signs of a nesting pair. The Merlin feeds mainly on small birds, captured after a short, fast chase.

Once the young have left the nest, the family group remains around the home island for a few weeks and then deserts the site in late summer as they follow the migration of small birds southward.

Earliest date:  April 7
Latest date:  October 19

# Peregrine Falcon

*Falco peregrinus*

Rare - Transient

It is unlikely this rare falcon is anything other than an occasional visitor to the area. The few records, including those made prior to the drastic population reduction in this species as a result of pesticide poisoning, appear to support this classification. Some of the more spectacular cliffs in Quetico on Kahshahpiwi and Agnes Lakes undoubtedly afford suitable nesting sites; what is lacking is a consistently reliable food source. Peregrines formerly nested along the Minnesota coast of Lake Superior, less than 112 km. southeast of Quetico Park.

Earliest date:  April 12
Latest date:  September 29

# Spruce Grouse

*Dendragapus canadensis*

Frequent - Permanent Resident

The Spruce Grouse is not an uncommon bird but it can be very difficult to find. The best places to look for the species are stands of young Jack Pine 20 to 40 feet in height. In Quetico, these areas are usually associated with burned over areas; out of the park, burns and cutovers create suitable habitat. In the spring, just as the snow is melting, the males drum to attract mates. A ground

Spruce Grouse

display with spread tail, erect neck feathers and enlarged bright red combs over each eye, is interspersed with short, noisy flights into a low tree branch. The muffled whirring of the wings can be heard for a considerable distance.

Spruce Grouse are often encountered on portages passing through Black Spruce bogs which are used as breeding sites if suitable Jack Pine areas are lacking. The birds are almost totally unafraid of man and usually only move aside to avoid being stepped on.

The fall is the best time to see Spruce Grouse. A

drive through old cutovers, for example in the Williamson Lake area north west of Atikokan in late September, will always be rewarded with good views of this grouse.

# Ruffed Grouse

*Bonasa umbellus*

Common - Permanent Resident

The Ruffed Grouse is commonly found throughout the park and the Atikokan area. Canoeists in the park usually see grouse on campsites or on portages. In the spring, the muffled drumming of the male grouse is a frequently heard but often unidentified sound. A quiet slow search will reveal the male grouse carefully watching you from his drumming log.

Several nests containing as many as 15 buff-coloured eggs are found each year by campers at French Lake in the northeast corner of Quetico Park. The eggs hatch in late May and early June and grouse of all sizes are a common feature of the campgrounds.

Unlike their wary relatives in southern Ontario, northern Ruffed Grouse are not afraid of man and can be closely approached.

In the winter, Ruffed Grouse can often be seen early in the morning and late in the evening, eating buds from the tops of birch and Trembling Aspen trees. They are quite agile as they climb about the thin branches plucking buds with a rapid peck and a twist of the head.

# Sharp-tailed Grouse

*Tympanuchus phasianellus*

Vagrant

There are no recent records of this impressive grouse in Quetico and only a few exist from outside the park. The area west of Fort Frances through to Rainy River is the place to find Sharp-tailed Grouse as the scrubby and semi-open farming country found in that area provides abundant suitable habitat. In the late 1930's and early 1940's Sharp-tailed Grouse were found in some numbers in the cutovers in the western section of the park. They apparently found the area unsuitable once regeneration and regrowth of the cutovers reached a certain stage. The Sharp-tailed Grouse seen in this area are the prairie subspecies.

# Yellow Rail

*Coturnicops noveboracensis*

Rare - Summer Resident

Although there have been several vague and intriguing reports of this rail in the past, two calling in a grass marsh in Atikokan, June 12, 1992, represent the only confirmed record.

# Virginia Rail

*Rallus limicola*

Rare - Summer Resident

There are no records of the Virginia Rail for Quetico, partly due to the lack of suitable cattail marsh habitat. Outside the park, records exist for the marshes at the mouth of the Atikokan River, Steep Rock Lake and the Auxiliary Rawn Reservoir. Two breeding records exist, both for the marsh at the mouth of the Atikokan River. One was a nest containing eggs and the other of newly hatched young.

Earliest date:  May 9
Latest date:  June 19

# Sora

*Porzana carolina*

Frequent - Summer Resident

The mouth of Deux Rivieres on Sturgeon Lake is a good place to hear this marsh-dwelling bird in Quetico. Seeing it is another question as it is very secretive. Again, the scarcity of suitable habitat in Quetico accounts for the general lack of records.

The large cattail marshes near the town of Atikokan support a good population of Soras. Their calls are a constant feature of the marshes but again, seeing the birds is a more difficult matter.

The Sora's "whinny" is the most frequently heard call but occasionally the questioning upwardly inflected "soree, soree" call, for which the bird is named, can be heard. The deeply cupped nest is carefully hidden in the rank marsh vegetation and is usually found only by accidently flushing the female.

Soras arrive in the spring as soon as the ice leaves the marshes. They have departed in the fall by the first heavy frosts in mid-September.

Earliest date:  May 9
Latest date:  September 14

## American Coot
*Fulica americana*

Uncommon - Summer Resident

The Coot has been recorded in Quetico only as a rare transient during the spring and fall migrations. Extensive marshes with adequate vegetative cover are almost non-existent in the park. All park records are for the spring and fall migration periods.

Outside Quetico, a few pairs of Coots nest each year in the cattail marshes near Atikokan. A slow paddle through the narrow channels between the stands of cattail will often be rewarded by a glimpse of this plump, dark gray, white-billed bird as it swims quickly away from the intruder.

It has a variety of calls, some strange and very unbird-like. The few nests discovered have all been carefully hidden in a clump of previous year's cattails, surrounded by open water.

Earliest date: April 21
Latest date: October

## Sandhill Crane
*Grus canadensis*

Rare - Transient

A few flocks or individuals of this impressive bird are usually recorded as they fly high overhead during the spring and fall migration periods. Their loud, far-carrying calls are what first attracts attention to the birds as they soar on outstretched wings. This is another species that breeds just west of Atikokan in the bogs of the Rainy River area. It is likely some flocks are mistaken for geese; the calls are similar and if the flock is high enough, the long trailing legs can be difficult to see.

Earliest date: April 11
Latest date: October 27

**NOTE:**
With the exception of the few species of shorebirds that nest in Quetico and the Atikokan area, shorebird records from year to year vary considerably and are directly related to habitat availability. Sandy beaches,

shallow lakes and mudflats, favoured feeding and resting areas for shorebirds, are uncommon in the area. Additionally, fluctuating water levels from year to year add or subtract significantly to available habitat. Thus, while a good overall number of shorebirds have been recorded, you cannot depend on the presence of any species in any given year. Good weather and limited habitat permit or force migrating shorebirds to simply fly right over the Atikokan area.

Formerly, the fluctuating water levels in Marmion Lake provided extensive mudflat habitat during the spring and fall migration periods and most shorebirds species were recorded there at one time or another. The stabilization of water levels in the lake has resulted in the loss of this locally important habitat.

## Black-bellied Plover

*Pluvialis squatarola*

Uncommon - Transient

This large plover is most frequently recorded during the fall migration. The mudflats on Marmion Lake, when exposed by low water levels, are a favourite resting and feeding site. Individuals in all plumage sequences, from full breeding dress, to the solid gray of winter, can be seen in a flock of a dozen individuals.

Occasionally, Black-bellied Plovers visit the open grassy areas in Atikokan but are less consistent than Lesser Golden-Plovers.

Earliest date:  May 18
Latest date:  October 11


# Lesser Golden-Plover
*Pluvialis dominica*

Uncommon - Transient

A few Lesser Golden-Plovers pass through the district each year. Spring records are greatly outnumbered by fall records. Surprisingly, the best place to see this bird is on the large lawns and school yards in the town of Atikokan. In mid-September flocks of 20 or more individuals can be watched as they deliberately and quietly walk about in the search for food.

They are a late fall migrant compared to other shorebirds and often linger in the area into October.

Earliest date:  May 18
Latest date:  October 11


# Semipalmated Plover
*Charadrius semipalmatus*

Uncommon - Transient

This small plover prefers open beaches and mudflats and is recorded in small numbers during the spring and fall migration periods.   It is usually noted singly or in small scattered flocks of three to six birds.

Earliest date: May 13
Latest date: September 13

## Piping Plover
*Charadrius melodus*

Vagrant

There is only one record in the Atikokan area of this endangered species. A single bird was observed May 13, 1978 on the mudflats of Marmion Lake.

Large isolated sand beaches preferred by this plover are not found in Quetico or the Atikokan area. However, a few pairs nest on the Sable Islands in the south-east corner of Lake of the Woods, 240 km. west of Atikokan. This location may be the last breeding site in Ontario.

## Killdeer
*Charadrius vociferus*

Frequent - Summer Resident

A very early spring migrant, the first Killdeer arrive while the lakes are still frozen and snow covers the land. The first birds somehow find tiny patches of open water and await more favourable conditions.

Killdeer breed infrequently in the park. The occasional pair will make use of a disturbed area such as an abandoned road or gravel pit, but, as these grow over with vegetation, the birds move to more suitable habitat. Each year several nests are found in the Atikokan area, usually in man-caused clearings. Sparsely vegetated, gravelly or sandy sites are preferred. The eggs, laid on the slightest excuse for a nest, blend perfectly with their surroundings and only by watching a pair of adult birds can the precise nest location be determined.

Earliest date:  March 30
Latest date:  September 29

## Greater Yellowlegs

*Tringa melanoleuca*

Frequent - Transient

The loud whistling cries of the Greater Yellowlegs are heard early in the spring, often when the only open water is along moving streams. It is a large shorebird and is apparently quite able to survive a few days of snow and cold as it awaits an opportunity to move northward.

In common with other shorebirds that nest in the far north, the last of what can be termed spring migrants in June are replaced by birds moving southward in mid-July. Greater Yellowlegs prefer open mudflats or shallow ponds on which to feed and rest. They quickly detect an intruder and immediately give the alarm,  hence their old name of "Tattler".

Earliest date:  April 13
Latest date:  October 16

# Lesser Yellowlegs
*Tringa flavipes*

Frequent - Transient

A smaller edition of the previous species, Lesser and Greater Yellowlegs are often found together during migration. They prefer the same habitats and care must be taken when identifying single birds. This species is decidedly more frequent during the fall migration period.

Earliest date:  April 20
Latest date:  September 30

# Solitary Sandpiper
*Tringa solitaria*

Uncommon - Transient

Records indicate this migrant is most often observed in the spring. Usually seen as individuals or pairs, Solitary Sandpipers prefer the edges of streams and smaller, well-sheltered ponds. They blend in remarkably well with their surroundings and often surprise the canoeist as they leap into flight with a loud whistle and a flash of their whitish rump and tail. With caution, the bird may be closely approached, allowing observation of the dark gray upper plumage that is spotted with tiny light-coloured dots. Solitaries occasionally bob up and down in the same manner as Spotted Sandpipers. During the spring, their loud calls are sometimes heard at night. Fall records are few. On June 22, 1987, an agitated Solitary Sandpiper was noted along the Beaver Meadows Trail at French Lake, in Quetico. It was seen again on July 2, 1987, and perhaps was breeding.

Earliest date:  April 31
Latest date:  October 10

## Willet
*Catoptrophorus semipalmatus*

Vagrant

A large light-gray shorebird with a startling black and white wing pattern was recorded on Turtle Lake north of Atikokan in the fall of 1978 and was undoubtedly this western species. Watch for it during the spring and fall migration periods.

## Spotted Sandpiper
*Actitis macularia*

Common - Summer Resident

As they travel the lakes and streams of the park, most canoeists will make the acquaintance of the "Spotty". This small sandpiper brings attention to itself by its piping calls and its interesting habit of bobbing up and down as it perches or walks about on a shoreline rock.

The female carefully hides her nest in low shoreline vegetation and if the four eggs are discovered, she puts on an impressive act to lure away the intruder. The eggs are large and the newly hatched young leave the nest as soon as their covering of down dries. They nimbly follow their mother in the never-ending search for food. The young are accomplished swimmers and do not hesitate to dive and swim away underwater if danger threatens.

Earliest date: April 20
Latest date: October 6

## Upland Sandpiper
*Bartramia longicauda*

Vagrant

The absence of extensive grassy fields or farmland precludes the presence of the Upland Sandpiper except as an occasional spring migrational stray. The three records for the area have all been of birds observed in the town of Atikokan, no doubt attracted to the school yards and lawns. This species breeds in the open farming country west of Fort Frances and our records are likely strays from there.

# Whimbrel

*Numenius phaeopus*

Vagrant

On June 1, 1977, a single bird was recorded on the Marmion Lake mudflats. A second individual, the first record for Quetico, remained most of the day on an exposed rock in French Lake on May 21, 1985.

# Hudsonian Godwit

*Limosa haemastica*

Vagrant

Two records for this impressive shorebird exist for the Atikokan area, both outside Quetico. On May 24, 1978 a breeding-plumaged individual was observed on the Marmion Lake mudflats. On May 20, 1987, two birds, one in breeding plumage and one in non-breeding plumage were found on Apungsisagen Lake. There are no fall records.

# Ruddy Turnstone

*Arenaria interpres*

Rare - Transient

There are only a handful of records for this remarkable shorebird in the park and in the Atikokan area.

Nearly all are of individuals in association with small mixed flocks of other migrating shorebirds. Small rocky islands, beaches and mudflats should be carefully checked during the migration periods for this species.

Earliest date: May 26
Latest date: August 27

## Red Knot
*Calidris canutus*

Vagrant

A single bird observed on the beach at the Lac la Croix park entry station is the only record for the area. The bird was recorded in early September of 1954.

## Sanderling
*Calidris alba*

Occasional - Transient

As its name implies, this is a shorebird of the beaches and open mudflats. Records for the park and the area have been made in the spring and the fall. Occasionally, a Sanderling is noted walking about lawns and schoolyards in Atikokan in the company of Lesser Golden-Plovers and Pectoral Sandpipers. Its white plumage stands out conspicuously against the background of green.

Earliest date: May 26
Latest date: September 26

## Semipalmated Sandpiper
*Calidris pusilla*

Uncommon - Transient

This sandpiper is the most common of the spring and fall shorebird migrants. On the more extensive beaches and mudflats of the area, flocks of 50 or more individuals have been recorded. It is a confiding little bird, allowing a close approach by the observer. It is frequently in the company of Least and Baird's Sandpipers, offering a good chance to compare a confusing group of species. During migration, individual birds of a flock vary greatly in their plumage and range from full breeding dress to full non-breeding plumage and, of course, every variation in between.

Earliest date:  May 11
Latest date:  September 13

## Least Sandpiper
*Calidris minutilla*

Uncommon - Transient

This is the smallest sandpiper to be seen in the area and also one of the most likely to be encountered. Where extensive beaches or mudflats exist, flocks of 40 or 50 individuals can be expected, both in the spring and the fall. Usually single birds, a pair or a small flock are noted. Small, bare, rocky islands in the larger lakes of the park, in addition to beaches, are favourite resting and feeding places. The tiny birds creep about rapidly as they search for food and give a very mouse-like impression.

Earliest date:  May 9
Latest date:  September 13

## White-rumped Sandpiper
*Calidris fuscicollis*

Rare - Transient

On June 4, 1974, a small flock of White-rumped Sandpipers was found in the Steep Rock Lake Marsh. The flock was resting on a floating stand of old cattails in the open part of the lake. It could easily be approached by canoe and the birds appeared to be very reluctant to move. All other records for this shorebird have occurred on the Marmion Lake mudflats and the French Lake beaches in Quetico.

Earliest date:  May 24
Latest date:  August 12

## Baird's Sandpiper
*Calidris bairdii*

Uncommon - Transient

A regular migrant both spring and fall on the Marmion Lake mudflats, this species has only been sparingly reported since the stabilization of water levels on the lake. Definitely preferring open beaches and mudflats, this bird should be watched for on French and Pickerel Lakes in Quetico.

Earliest date: May 21
Latest date: September 13

## Pectoral Sandpiper

*Calidris melanotos*

Uncommon - Transient

This medium-sized sandpiper is recorded each year in small numbers during both the spring and fall migration periods. It has been noted in a variety of shoreline habitats - beaches, mudflats, small rocky islands and sedgy marshes. It has also been observed on lawns and schoolyards in Atikokan, frequently in company with Lesser Golden-Plovers.

Earliest date: May 14
Latest date: October 14

## Dunlin

*Calidris alpina*

Rare - Transient

Quetico and the Atikokan area appear to be well off the main migration routes for this sandpiper. Only half a dozen records have been made on a variety of habitats including beaches, mudflats, bare rocky islands and short grass marshes.

Earliest date:  May 11
Latest date:  September 25

## Stilt Sandpiper

*Calidris himantopus*

Rare - Transient

Only a few fall records have been made for this species.  All Lesser Yellowlegs, both individuals and flocks, should be carefully scanned for this species - it is quite similar in appearance and habits.  This sandpiper prefers muddy areas rather than beaches and should be looked for during the fall migration period.

Earliest date:  August 3
Latest date:  September 1

## Buff-breasted Sandpiper

*Tryngites subruficollis*

Rare - Transient

All records for this pretty sandpiper have occurred during the fall migration period on the Marmion Lake mudflats.  On the open flats the birds have an interesting and characteristic way of picking up their feet as they walk. Perhaps this is an adaptation for moving through low vegetation, the Buff-breasted Sandpiper's preferred habitat. Most records have occurred during the first half of September. In Quetico, look for this species on any large beach during early September.

Earliest date: July 22
Latest date: September 13


## Short-billed Dowitcher

*Limnodromus griseus*

Occasional - Transient

This large chunky shorebird is usually recorded in small groups of two to four individuals. Its size, long bill and manner of feeding make it quite conspicuous. While occasionally seen on beaches, it is partial to mudflats and the muddy edges of lakes during periods of low water levels. Here it can probe the soft mud for food.

Earliest date: May 12
Latest date: September 5

# Common Snipe
*Gallinago gallinago*

Frequent - Summer Resident

Most marshy areas of any size will have a pair of Common Snipe in residence. The winnowing flights of the male are a characteristic sound of the spring and summer marshes. The wavering sound that rises up at the end is easily noticed by park visitors but not so easily identified or even associated with a bird. Snipe are early spring migrants and can sometimes be noted very late in the fall. There is one winter record of a single bird that managed to survive along the banks of a small trickle of open water.

Earliest date: April 13
Latest date: October 20

# American Woodcock
*Scolopax minor*

Frequent - Summer Resident

Patches of snow still linger in the bush when the first Woodcock return in the spring. The birds seek out moist areas with a covering of alder, willow and aspen, preferably with a few small grassy clearings. Almost immediately, males establish territories and start the elaborate business of attracting a mate. Shortly after sunset, the evening quiet will be punctuated by an unusual short buzzy call, repeated every few seconds. This is followed by a whir of wings and, if there is enough light, a small thickset, long-billed bird can be seen spiralling upward into the sky. After a few circles in the air, the bird pitches to earth accompanied by musical chirping notes and then immediately resumes the ground call.

For several years in the 1980's a pair of Woodcock held a territory at the old Naturalists' Building at French Lake. The male was totally unafraid of people and was not the least bit reluctant to carry out his territorial display in front of an audience.

Earliest date:  April 3
Latest date:  October 13

## Wilson's Phalarope

*Phalaropus tricolor*

Rare - Transient

The Wilson's Phalarope breeds just west of Atikokan in the Rainy River area.  In spite of this, there are few records for Quetico and Atikokan.  It has been observed on the Marmion Lake mudflats and in the marsh at the mouth of the Atikokan River.

Earliest date:  May 5
Latest date:  June 5

# Red-necked Phalarope
*Phalaropus lobatus*

Rare - Transient

Even less frequently encountered than the previous species, all records for the Red-necked Phalarope have been made in the early fall. Phalaropes often frequent deep water, spinning in little circles as they feed. They can be expected almost anywhere in the park and the Atikokan area.

Earliest date:  August 4
Latest date:  September 1

# Parasitic Jaeger
*Stercorarius parasiticus*

Vagrant

On September 1, 1977, two Parasitic Jaegers were observed on Clearwater West Lake, a large lake about 25 miles northwest of Atikokan.

The overland migration patterns of jaegers are poorly understood. Canoeists travelling the larger lakes of the park in late August and early September should be aware that seeing a jaeger is a possibility.

# Bonaparte's Gull

*Larus philadelphia*

Occasional - Transient

Recorded only during the spring and fall migration periods, this small gull is not a regular visitor to the area. Spring is the most likely time of year for it to occur and its appearance usually coincides with the final ice breakup on the larger lakes. Small flocks of these black-headed birds have been observed resting quietly on drifting pieces of ice and usually allow a close approach.

Earliest date: May 9
Latest date: September 10

# Ring-billed Gull

*Larus delawarensis*

Occasional - Transient

There are only a few spring records for this gull. In late summer and early fall, it is more frequently encountered, particularly on the larger lakes. There appears to be a post-breeding dispersal of adults and young into the area and large flocks can regularly be seen on Clearwater West Lake in late August and early September. Smaller groups have also been recorded on other large lakes such as Marmion Lake. There is no evidence this species breeds in the area.

Earliest date: April 25
Latest date: October 10

# Herring Gull

*Larus argentatus*

Common - Summer Resident

One of the early spring migrants, Herring Gulls are usually heard before they are seen.  Their loud cries echo across the frozen lakes as they stand on the ice and announce to the world they have arrived.  Often calls will drift downward from small flocks of birds that are slowly moving northward high in the air.

Herring Gulls breed throughout the park and the Atikokan area and most lakes of any size have a few resident pairs.  Large breeding colonies are few; however, one on an island in Wolseley Lake in the west end of Quetico and one on Calm Lake are noteworthy.  Generally a single pair or two will use a small rocky island for a nest site.  Occupied islands are vigorously defended by the adults who fly out to any approaching visitors.

The dark-coloured young are on the wing by mid-summer.  Adults are still in the area in mid-November but disappear soon after as the lakes finally freeze up.

Earliest date:  March 24
Latest date:  November 27

# Caspian Tern

*Sterna caspia*

Vagrant

A single bird, flying strongly eastward over Pickerel Lake on June 30, 1981, was the only record for this large tern in Quetico until another was seen on the same lake July 30, 1993.

# Common Tern

*Sterna hirundo*

Uncommon - Summer Resident

Although this tern is frequently noted on the larger park lakes during migration, no breeding has been confirmed for Quetico. Several small colonies have been located on lakes in the north part of the Atikokan area, including one on White Otter Lake that contains about 25 pairs. In all cases, a small rocky island has been chosen for the colony site.

Earliest date:  May 15
Latest date:  August 21

# Forster's Tern

*Sterna forsteri*

Vagrant

The one record for the area, by Nash and Bray, occurred May 9, 1979, in the Steep Rock Lake Marsh, an appropriate place for this marsh-dwelling species. All white terns encountered in the park and the rest of the Atikokan area should be carefully observed in case they are this species.

# Black Tern

*Chlidonias niger*

Uncommon - Summer Resident

The large marshy areas required by this tern for breeding are very scarce in the area. Park records involve migrating birds only and no confirmation of breeding has occurred. Outside Quetico, the large marshes in Steep Rock Lake, at the mouth of the Atikokan River and the Auxiliary Rawn Reservoirs support breeding colonies. About 10 pair use the Steep Rock Lake marshes and build their small nests on small mounds of floating vegetation, surrounded by cattails. The colony vigorously defends the nesting area, diving and screaming at the intruder incessantly.

The young terns are on the wing by mid-July when

they leave the area with the adults, not to be seen until the following spring.

Earliest date: May 14
Latest date: July 5

## Mourning Dove

*Zenaida macroura*

Uncommon - Summer Resident

Most records for the Mourning Dove have been made in the general area of the town of Atikokan. The open areas of the town with scattered trees are attractive to the species and the presence of birds throughout the summer indicates breeding. Park records are more irregular and appear to include primarily migrating birds that have wandered.

Earliest date: April 18
Latest date: October 4

## Inca Dove

*Scardafella inca*

Vagrant

On October 7, 1992, an Inca Dove was found on the train tracks west of Atikokan near Caribus Creek. It remained in the area for seven days. Normally found in southern Texas and Arizona, this amazing record was the first for Canada and Ontario.

# Black-billed Cuckoo

*Coccyzus erythropthalmus*

Uncommon - Summer Resident

The first indication of the Black-billed Cuckoo's return in the spring is the sound of its characteristic call coming from a bushy tangle of vegetation. It is quite secretive and is likely more common than existing records indicate. It appears to favour the bushy conditions along the edges of streams and rivers and should be looked and listened for in these areas.

It is an interesting fact that a surprising number of cuckoo nests are found each fall after the vegetation is free of leaves. This is another indication the species is here in reasonable numbers.

Earliest date: May 13
Latest date: September 6

# Yellow-billed Cuckoo

*Coccyzus americanus*

Vagrant

There are three records for this cuckoo, none of which were made in Quetico. The first, near Atikokan, was recorded June 15, 1963. The second observation was at Forsberg Lake, July 12, 1979 and the third at the Atikokan Municipal Airport on July 17, 1983.

## Eastern Screech-Owl

*Otus asio*

Vagrant

For two consecutive years, on May 31, 1974 and May 24, 1975, a Screech-Owl was heard calling in Atikokan in the river valley. The riparian habitat is suited for the species but the above-noted records remain unique.

## Great Horned Owl

*Bubo virginianus*

Uncommon - Permanent Resident

Anytime after mid-February the Great Horned Owl starts to call. The hollow, booming hoots carry far in the cold still air of the Quetico night. This owl uses raven nests in trees as breeding sites and will return year after year, if not disturbed, until the nest disintegrates and falls. As in other parts of its Ontario range, breeding starts very early in the year, long before the snow is gone.

Occasionally, in winter, very light-coloured individuals have been noted, indicating a southward movement of birds from much farther north.

# Snowy Owl

*Nyctea scandiaca*

Rare - Winter Visitor

The Snowy Owl is an irregular visitor to the area. During some winters, several sightings will be made and then none will occur for a number of years.

# Northern Hawk Owl

*Surnia ulula*

Rare - Permanent Resident

The first breeding record for this day-flying owl occurred in 1972 near Zephira Lake in the northeastern corner of Quetico. A family of recently fledged young was noted with an adult bird. Fledged young were again noted in August of 1979 near Seashore Lake in the north part of the Atikokan area.

Fall and winter records are made each year and likely include birds that have moved in from more northern locations. Northern Hawk Owls show little concern for man and usually allow a close approach. They favour open areas, so old cutovers and burned areas should be carefully scanned, both in the summer and in the winter.

# Barred Owl

*Strix varia*

Frequent - Permanent Resident

This is the owl most likely to be seen or heard in Quetico. It is a vocal species and its characteristic call of eight hoots can be heard throughout the year. Barred Owls have a large vocabulary and many strange night sounds can be attributed to them. The birds frequently visit campsites in Quetico, no doubt attracted by small rodents that have in turn been attracted by bits of food left by campers. It can be quite startling when two owls hold a conversation above your tent in the middle of the night. While they feed chiefly on rodents, one was observed catching large moths that had been attracted to the gatehouse lights at French Lake.

Occasionally, a Barred Owl will be observed sitting on a utility pole in full daylight. This usually occurs in the winter when the birds must spend more time to secure food.

**Barred Owl**

# Great Gray Owl

*Strix nebulosa*

Rare - Permanent Resident

This huge owl is always a delight and a surprise to see. Winter is perhaps the best time to look for it, particularly along the bush roads of the area in cutovers along Highway 11.

A number of summer records made over the years indicated the possibility of breeding. This was confirmed in a rather unusual way. A study of Great Gray Owls was conducted in northern Minnesota in 1980. A number of birds were captured and fitted with small radio units for tracing. In 1981 a major exodus of owls from the study area occurred, apparently as a result of a decline in the small rodent population. As the researchers extended their area of search for the owls, a radio signal was picked up near Hardtack Lake, just north of Atikokan. The bird was finally located and proved to be a female, still carrying her radio. She was sitting on a nest containing 2 eggs high up in a Jack Pine. The same bird had hatched and fledged five young the spring before in Minnesota.

Like the Northern Hawk Owl, Great Gray Owls are active during the day and also allow an observer to approach them closely.

# Long-eared Owl

*Asio otus*

Rare - Transient

The few records for this owl indicate that it rarely occurs in the district. Three of the four records have been of injured or dead birds, hit by cars during the spring and fall migration periods. While the extensive forests of the area apparently do not provide suitable habitat for the species, a pair engaged in territorial flight May 3, 1992 near the Hardy Dam indicated breeding may occur occasionally.

Earliest date: April 8
Latest date: October 10

# Short-eared Owl

*Asio flammeus*

Rare - Transient

This owl is apparently only a visiting migrant to the area during the spring and the fall. The open habitat preferred by the species is not present in the area. There are no records for Quetico. On May 5, 1991, three individuals were recorded hunting over the short grass marsh at Caribus Creek.

Earliest date: April 12
Latest date: October 28

# Boreal Owl

*Aegolius funereus*

Rare - Permanent Resident

The call of the male Boreal Owl is very similar to the flight sound (winnowing) of the Common Snipe. Until this was known, records for the Boreal Owl in this area consisted of occasional birds accidentally caught in traps during the winter trapping season.

In 1976 an owl started calling at French Lake on January 24. Calling continued intermittently through to March, always in the same area. Each year since, a Boreal Owl has called at this site. Others have been heard in the Sapawe area.

The male apparently calls only until a mate is attracted. The time spent calling may thus be long or short, depending on the availability of a female.

While still considered a rare bird, it is likely the Boreal Owl is found in small numbers throughout the Atikokan area and is more common than supposed. Studies carried out in northeastern Minnesota where several nest sites have been found in recent years appear to bear this out.

# Northern Saw-whet Owl

*Aegolius acadicus*

Uncommon - Permanent Resident

This tiny owl can most easily be found by following its characteristic call heard in the park from early February to mid-summer. A calling male will usually respond quickly to an imitation of his call and provide the birder with a look at the bird. For several years a pair nested in a large Red Pine near the picnic shelter at French Lake. Another pair nested in a large Trembling Aspen behind the Beaverhouse Lake entry station. In both cases old Pileated Woodpecker holes were used by the owls.

Saw-whets do not appear to have specific habitat requirements and have been observed everywhere in the Atikokan area from mature forest to open cutovers and burns. The presence of a suitable nest cavity and a food source is the basic requirement.

The migrational pattern of the species is not well understood. Since birds have been recorded all winter and males start calling in mid-February, there is a definite resident population. However, several have been captured and banded during the first week in October and perhaps indicate a migration of birds from further north. A similar movement in the spring is not evident.

# Common Nighthawk

*Chordeiles minor*

Frequent - Summer Resident

Except as migrants, Common Nighthawks are only occasionally seen in Quetico. The open areas they prefer are scarce, and suitable breeding habitat is limited to recently burned areas and patches of bare bedrock. Outside the park, recent cutovers are used by the birds and there is usually a pair or two in each cutover. Nests are often found by tree-planting crews, the eggs simply laid in a slight hollow in the ground. The female, eggs and young blend perfectly into their surroundings and nests are only discovered by accidentally flushing the female.

Earliest date:  May 15
Latest date:  September 8

# Whip-poor-will

*Caprimulgus vociferus*

Occasional - Summer Resident

The Whip-poor-will has been mainly recorded from the southern portion of Quetico Park and seems to be associated with the aspen and mixed woodlands of that area. There are very few records for the more northerly parts of the park and the Atikokan area. One of the earliest written records of a bird in the park was made by

Bigsby in 1823. In his book "Shoe and Canoe" the call of the Whip-poor-will kept his camp entertained all night.

What the status of the bird is after it ceases calling in late July is not known.

Earliest date: May 15
Latest date: July 23


## Chimney Swift

*Chaetura pelagica*

Occasional - Transient and Summer Resident

Although this species is a common breeding bird in the town of Fort Frances just 144 km. to the west, it is very uncommon in the park and the Atikokan area. Most records appear to be of wandering migrants or non-breeding birds and are most likely to be seen in or around the town of Atikokan, probably attracted by the buildings.

Since 1982, several pairs of Chimney Swifts have been present in Atikokan throughout the summer. It appears they breed in several large chimneys in the town.

Earliest date: May 7
Latest date: August 15

# Ruby-throated Hummingbird

*Archilochus colubris*

Frequent - Summer Resident

In Quetico, this tiny bird is likely more common than records indicate. Its small size and rapid movements make observation difficult. Stands of Jewel Weed in bloom along lake shores and the edges of beaver ponds are particularly attractive to hummingbirds. Several park entry station attendants maintain hummingbird feeders and quickly attract a pair of birds. The resident pair is very possessive of their territory and drive away all other hummingbirds that trespass.

In the town of Atikokan, the flower gardens and feeders attract a number of hummingbirds. Each year more and more people maintain feeders and enjoy watching the tiny visitors.

Earliest date: May 8
Latest date: October 18

# Rufous Hummingbird

*Selasphorus rufus*

Vagrant

The first and only record for this western hummingbird in this area was made at Sapawe, 25 km. east of Atikokan on September 15, 1983. The bird came to a feeder and was present for several days.


# Belted Kingfisher

*Ceryle alcyon*

Frequent - Summer Resident

Except during migration, when they may be found anywhere along the area's lakes and rivers, kingfishers are found only where an exposed vertical bank of soil provides a nesting site. The birds will find and use gravel and sand pits, road cuts or the banks of lakes and streams. Often they find suitable sites a long distance from the water.

The canoeist often sees kingfishers when the birds fly with a loud rattling call from a perch overhanging the water. Kingfishers are sometimes observed hovering over water with rapidly beating wings and downward-pointed bill. If prey is sighted, the bird drops like a stone and hits the water with a splash. It soon emerges, and with a shake of its feathers to remove water, it flies quickly to a perch to swallow its prey.

Earliest date: April 13
Latest date: October 29

## Red-headed Woodpecker
*Melanerpes erythrocephalus*

Vagrant

Only two records for this attractive woodpecker exist for the area, one in Quetico and one just north of the park near Beaverhouse Lake. Both records were made in mid-summer. They appear to be wandering non-breeding birds. The Red-headed Woodpecker nests in the Rainy River area, west of Fort Frances.

## Yellow-bellied Sapsucker
*Sphyrapicus varius*

Common - Summer Resident

Around the middle of April, the first sapsuckers return to the park. The forest soon rings with their calls and characteristic drumming - a fast roll followed by several spaced single taps. Nest holes are started and are usually chiselled in living Trembling Aspen. Park visitors often notice birch, alder, Balsam Fir and other trees ringed by a cluster of small squarish holes. Sapsuckers are responsible for this and feed from the sap that oozes from the holes. They also eat insects that are attracted to the sap.

Earliest date: March 29
Latest date: October 14

**Yellow-Bellied Sapsucker**

# Downy Woodpecker
*Picoides pubescens*

Frequent - Permanent Resident

The smallest of the area's resident woodpeckers, the Downy Woodpecker is liable to be encountered anywhere during the year. They are frequent visitors to feeders in winter where fat or suet are provided on a regular basis. The Downy is another of the woodpeckers that often uses a living Trembling Aspen in which to nest. The nest chamber is dug out in early May and the young of the year are often on the wing by early July. Banding records indicate the species is resident, remaining in a given area throughout the year.

# Hairy Woodpecker
*Picoides villosus*

Frequent - Permanent Resident

This woodpecker can usually be found almost anywhere, but in small numbers. It is a common feeder visitor and several may use a feeding station during the winter. In early February, the males become aggressive and will start to display if they encounter each other or a female.

The Hairy Woodpecker generally digs a nest

chamber in a live Trembling Aspen. The site chosen is often on the edge of a clearing and once the young are partly grown, their loud calls attract attention to the nest. The nest is seldom less than seven meters from the ground.

## Three-toed Woodpecker
*Picoides tridactylus*

Occasional - Permanent Resident

. Found in much the same areas as the Black-backed Woodpecker, this species is much less frequently observed. To see it, the observer should concentrate on searching recent burns and listen for the sounds of quiet tapping. Both this species and the Black-backed Woodpecker frequently nest in living conifers, such as Jack Pine or spruce.

A definite movement of birds occurs through the park and the area during October.

Once a Three-toed Woodpecker has been found, it is very easy to watch, allowing a close approach and normally paying not the slightest attention to the observer.

# Black-backed Woodpecker
*Picoides arcticus*

Uncommon - Permanent Resident

Although this woodpecker can be found almost anywhere, the best places to look are in recently burned areas or in spruce or Tamarack stands that have been killed by beaver ponds. Dead trees appear to lose their attractiveness to the species after a couple of years. Perhaps the insects found under the bark of recently dead trees are no longer present after a certain length of time.

Black-backs are not noisy and often the only indication of their presence is the sound of gentle tapping as they flake the bark from the trunk of a tree. In winter, the birds will stay in a suitable stand of dead trees for long periods of time and can be found day after day.

There is a definite movement of this woodpecker during the month of October and more are observed then than at any other time of the year.

# Northern Flicker
*Colaptes auratus*

Common - Summer Resident

Spring has definitely arrived when the call of the Flicker is heard throughout the park. Found throughout Quetico and the Atikokan area, it is the most frequently encountered woodpecker. Standing dead trees in beaver ponds are favoured nesting sites. Over the years they will dig a number of nest holes and as long as the tree stands, other birds such as Tree Swallows take over the ones abandoned by the Flickers.

Earliest date:  April 10
Latest date:  November 1

## Pileated Woodpecker

*Dryocopus pileatus*

Frequent - Resident

This impressive woodpecker is found throughout Quetico and the Atikokan area.  It seems to have increased in numbers in the past 10 years.

Territorial establishment starts in March when the males announce their presence with loud flicker-like calls. Pairs appear to remain in their home area throughout the year.

Nest cavities are usually built in large live Trembling Aspen at a substantial height above the ground. New cavities are often built each year, the abandoned ones being used by other birds and animals such as Northern Saw-whet Owls and Northern Flying Squirrels.  The young are quite vocal and draw attention to the nest site with their calls for food.

# Olive-sided Flycatcher

*Contopus borealis*

Uncommon - Summer Resident

Were it not for its loud "hip - three cheers" call, this boreal flycatcher would go largely unnoticed. Its habit of sitting in plain sight at the very top of a dead tree and calling loudly between short insect-catching flights attracts the attention of the birder. It is not a common bird and seems to prefer the edges of lakes, rivers and beaver ponds. The dead trees and open space, particularly in and around beaver ponds, are apparently to its liking.

The Olive-sided Flycatcher is not an early spring arrival and it may be the first week in June before it is seen.

As with many other birds of the area, its late summer and fall movements southward are undertaken in silence and it leaves the park largely unnoticed.

Earliest date:  May 21
Latest date:  September 10

# Eastern Wood-Pewee

*Contopus virens*

Uncommon - Summer Resident

This inconspicuous forest flycatcher is found sparingly throughout the area. It favours stands of mature

Jack Pine and mixed forest where aspen and birch are growing in association with White Spruce and Balsam Fir.

The first indication of its presence is its gentle call from which it receives its common name.

Earliest date:  May 18
Latest date:  September 15

## Yellow-bellied Flycatcher
*Empidonax flaviventris*

Uncommon - Summer Resident

This small flycatcher frequents Black Spruce bogs and mature mixed forest.  It is an inconspicuous bird and does not bring attention to its presence with a loud song or brilliant plumage.

Often the first indication of its presence is its soft "chebok" call, deeper and less frequently repeated than the "chebek" call of its relative, the Least Flycatcher.  Once the call is noted, a careful stalk will be rewarded with a glimpse of the bird.  It frequently makes long flights in pursuit of insects, seldom returning to the same perch from which it started its flight.  It is one of the few flycatchers that hides its nest on the forest floor.

Earliest date:  May 17
Latest date:  August 29

# Alder Flycatcher

*Empidonax alnorum*

Common - Summer Resident

The Alder Flycatcher can easily be found throughout the park and the Atikokan area in clumps of alders and willows that grow along the shores of lakes, streams, marshes and swamps. It is easily approachable although difficult to see in the thick vegetation of its habitat. It is a rather late spring arrival and its calls, usually the first indication of its presence, are a characteristic sound of canoe country.

The rather bulky nest is placed at no great height in alders or other shrubbery.

Earliest date: May 15
Latest date: August 29

# Least Flycatcher

*Empidonax minimus*

Common - Summer Resident

The smallest of the "Empidonax" group of flycatchers found in the area, the Least Flycatcher favours mature deciduous or mixed forest. It attracts attention to its presence with its emphatic, often repeated call note, "chebek, chebek". It is an active species, dashing about in pursuit of insect food or chasing its mate and intruding neighbours. Nests are usually placed in a branch fork at a good height in a birch or aspen. The skilful use of lichens as camouflage make the nest particularly hard to see.

Earliest date:  May 11
Latest date:  September 3

Gisela © '93

## Alder Flycatcher

# Eastern Phoebe
*Sayornis phoebe*

Uncommon - Summer Resident

Phoebes are, at best, widely scattered throughout the park and the Atikokan area. Once a nesting site has been found however, there is a tendency for a pair to return to it year after year. They are attracted by the activities of man; sheds, outbuildings and bridges are favourite breeding sites - as they are in other parts of its range. Occasionally a pair will be found in a remote area, far from any evidence of man's presence. There the birds will nest in a small niche in a waterside cliff. One such site is located in the Namakan Narrows, between Sandpoint Lake and Namakan Lake. The birds have used the site for many years and several old nests can be found in tiny cavities in the cliff, a few feet above the water line.

Earliest date:  April 29
Latest date:  September 3

# Say's Phoebe
*Sayornis saya*

Vagrant

Only one record for this western species exists for the area. A single bird was observed in the town of Atikokan on May 27, 1960 by Peruniak.

## Great Crested Flycatcher

*Myiarchus crinitus*

Rare - Summer Resident

This impressive flycatcher is on the very northern edge of its range in Quetico Park and the Atikokan area.

Most records have been made in the town of Atikokan along the Atikokan River and it has nested several times in boxes erected for Wood Ducks.

It is not difficult to find if it is around; its loud ringing cries immediately attract attention.

Earliest date:  May 18
Latest date:  September 17


## Eastern Kingbird

*Tyrannus tyrannus*

Frequent - Summer Resident

Kingbirds are usually one of the later migrants to return to Quetico in the spring.  It is often early June before the last ones have arrived.

Small beaver ponds with water-killed trees attract this flycatcher and the nest is usually placed at no great height in the branches of a dead tree.

Kingbirds are noisy, aggressive birds and readily attract attention to themselves. They do not hesitate to attack and chase much larger birds. They can make life quite miserable for hawks such as the Broad-winged Hawk if it has a territory coincident with the kingbird.

Most kingbirds have left the area by mid-September, moving southward in family groups.

Earliest date:  May 8
Latest date:  August 27

## Horned Lark
*Eremophila alpestris*

Uncommon - Spring and Fall Transient

The Horned Lark does not breed in the park or the Atikokan area. It can be observed in both the spring and the fall during migration. Beaches, rocky points and islands attract it, as do the open fields, schoolyards and weedy roadsides in Atikokan.

It is an early migrant and has been noted along roads and highways on the patches of gravel exposed by snow ploughs, long before the spring melt has started. Likewise, it will linger in the fall into November. It is a confiding bird and will allow a close approach if the birder is careful.

Earliest date:  March 25
Latest date:  November 3

# Purple Martin

*Progne subis*

Uncommon - Summer Resident

This magnificent colonial swallow is only regularly found in the very southwest corner of the Atikokan area. It is another species that is common from Fort Frances west but does not, except occasionally, visit Quetico or the Atikokan area. Park records are of small groups moving high overhead during migration. In Atikokan a pair or two of birds are usually noted each year, apparently attracted by the numerous bird houses. There never seem to be enough to initiate a nesting colony. Many cottagers on Sandpoint and Namakan Lakes have nesting boxes suitable for Purple Martins and enjoy the presence of a breeding colony each year.

Earliest date:  May 19
Latest date:  August 20

# Tree Swallow

*Tachycineta bicolor*

Common - Summer Resident

This is the first swallow to arrive in the spring and quite often appears before all the snow has gone and the lakes are still ice-covered. In Quetico the Tree Swallow seeks out abandoned woodpecker holes and natural cavities in dead trees in which to nest. Thus it is one of the birds frequently seen around beaver ponds. In Atikokan it takes advantage of bird houses in residential yards and is a common sight in the town.

Although it is the first swallow to arrive in the spring, it is also the first to leave after nesting. The young are fledged by late July and a complete exodus of the species follows. Observing a Tree Swallow in the park and surrounding area after early August is unusual.

Earliest date: March 31
Latest date: September 2

## Northern Rough-winged Swallow
*Stelgidopteryx serripennis*

Rare - Summer Resident

One or two pairs of this swallow are usually recorded in the area each year. Since it is not a colonial species, it can utilize small exposed soil banks in which to nest. Any solitary pair of swallows noticed along the edges of lakes and streams where earth banks exist, should be very carefully checked in case they are Northern Rough-winged Swallows.

Earliest date: May 13
Latest date: July 20

# Bank Swallow
*Riparia riparia*

Uncommon - Summer Resident

This colonial swallow, except during migration, is not found in Quetico. No doubt the complete absence of suitable exposed earth banks accounts for this.

Elsewhere in the Atikokan area, colonies, often of considerable size (100 pair), find and use earth banks created by commercial gravel removals. The birds are quick to find and utilize newly opened pits. In common with the Tree Swallow, it moves southward during mid-August.

Earliest date: April 25
Latest date: August 26

# Cliff Swallow
*Hirundo pyrrhonota*

Common - Summer Resident

As with the Barn Swallow, this colonial species tends to use man-made structures as nesting sites. Most park records are of migrating birds although a large colony nested on a large building in a logging camp for many years until the building was removed. In Atikokan its mud nests are a common sight under the eaves of stores and houses.

When they are building their nests and feeding young, a colony is a busy sight with a constant coming and going of birds.

Earliest date: April 30
Latest date: August 27

## Barn Swallow

*Hirundo rustica*

Common - Summer Resident

This swallow is quick to utilize man-made structures such as buildings and bridges for nesting sites. In Quetico such features are practically non-existent so Barn Swallow records for the park consist almost entirely of spring and fall migrants. Very occasionally a pair resort to a natural nesting site and will use a lakeside overhanging cliff.

Elsewhere in the district, the birds are found wherever a suitable nesting structure is available. Along Highway 11 every wooden culvert is home to a pair.

Barn Swallows are the last of the swallows to leave the area in the fall.

Earliest date: April 28
Latest date: September 1

## Gray Jay

*Perisoreus canadensis*

Common - Permanent Resident

Canoeists in Quetico invariably make the acquaintance of this bird on a lakeside campsite. Arriving silently with a glide into a nearby tree, the jay quickly identifies all sources of food and will help itself to whatever is available, whether it is offered by the camper or not.

Gray Jays are friendly and confiding. They quickly learn to take food from the hands of people. For a jay they are gentle and quiet. However, they have a wide variety of calls, some loud and harsh, some soft and musical.

Nests are built in early March, usually in a conifer and are constructed of warm insulating materials such as soft fibre from cattail heads. The dark gray young are on the wing about the time most other summer breeding birds are just arriving from the south.

## Blue Jay

*Cyanocitta cristata*

Common - Permanent Resident

Noisy and bright coloured, the Blue Jay seems to go out of its way to be sure its presence is noted. There is a definite spring and fall movement of the birds and it is possible those wintering in the area are not the same ones that nest.

They soon find feeders during the winter and while they eat some food, most of their efforts are directed to taking mouthfuls away to be hidden, apparently for later use. Sunflower seeds are favourites, the birds holding the seed firmly with both feet, striking it repeatedly with the bill until the hull is split. Blue Jays lose their characteristic noisiness during their nesting period and become quiet, secretive birds. After the breeding season they quickly revert to the norm.

## Black-billed Magpie

*Pica pica*

Rare - Winter Visitor

This spectacular black and white visitor from the west is usually recorded in the area every winter. The numbers of birds noted are variable; on the 1975 Christmas Bird Count for Atikokan three were present at the Atikokan town landfill site. Landfill sites attract the birds and they tend to stay around them if not disturbed. They are very shy however, and usually fly some distance if encountered.

Since 1980, Black-billed Magpies have nested in the Rainy River area, 240 km. west of Atikokan, using clumps of willows in which to place their large, domed stick nest.

# American Crow

*Corvus brachyrhynchos*

Common - Summer Resident

The American Crow, although preferring more open country, is found throughout Quetico and the Atikokan area.

Crows enjoy the singular distinction of being the first of the spring migrants to return, usually during the first week of March. The newly returned birds are very vocal but are hard-pressed to find enough to eat in the frozen and snow-covered park.

In Atikokan they are common birds in the residential areas, frequenting lawns and parks and being quite tolerant of man. This is in marked contrast with other areas where years of persecution have made them wary and distrustful.

Crows have an extreme dislike for Common Ravens during the nesting season and never hesitate to drive the larger birds away.

A few American Crows usually winter in Atikokan each year but most move south into the mid-western United States.

Earliest date: March 3
Latest date: December 31

# Common Raven

*Corvus corax*

Common - Permanent Resident

Visitors to Quetico and the Atikokan area who have never been to the "north" invariably comment on the size of the "crows" they encounter. They are, of course, seeing Common Ravens for the first time. Ravens are a common sight to the canoeist and nothing is more thrilling than watching these masters of the air winging across the face of cliffs, giving voice to their raucous calls.

Ravens use a variety of nest sites. Cliffside nests are the most spectacular and the easiest to watch. The bulky stick nest is also placed in a large tree, usually a Jack Pine or a Trembling Aspen. Nest sites are used year after year and some cliff nests reach a very large size.

Young Common Ravens are out of the nest by mid-June and the family group remains together for some time.

In January, when the land is firmly locked in winter's grip, ravens begin to pair although birds are not observed carrying nesting material until early March.

# Black-capped Chickadee
*Parus atricapillus*

Common - Permanent Resident

This is one of the few birds that remain in Quetico for the winter and its friendliness is most welcome to the snowshoer or skier on the move through the snowy silences of the park. As the sun slowly increases in strength after the short days of December, Black-capped Chickadees can be heard giving their characteristic "spring's here" call note. Once the snow is gone in mid-April, pairs can be found excavating nesting sites in dead stubs. A birch or aspen stub of no great diameter is usually selected, the main requirement being the state of decay. The stub must be rotten enough to permit the birds to chip out a cavity but strong enough not to fall over. The birds take turns digging and carrying the chips away, never leaving them to accumulate at the base of the nest stub.

The Black-capped Chickadee is a regular visitor to feeders in the winter and soon becomes tame enough to take food from the hand.

# Boreal Chickadee
*Parus hudsonicus*

Frequent - Permanent Resident

The Boreal Chickadee inhabits mature stands of Black Spruce. Its nasal "chickadee" call is usually the first indication of its presence. It is not as noisy a bird as the

Black-capped Chickadee and can easily be overlooked.

As occasional winter visitors to feeders, Boreals prefer bread and suet to other foods. Interestingly enough it rarely eats sunflower seeds, a favourite of the Black-cap.

The nest is placed in a cavity in a rotten spruce stub, excavated by the birds in April.

Boreal Chickadee

# Red-breasted Nuthatch

*Sitta canadensis*

Common - Permanent Resident

The Red-breasted Nuthatch is frequently found in mature coniferous and mixed wood forests throughout Quetico. Canoeists will usually hear its tinny "ank ank" call before they notice the tiny bird creeping energetically up, down and sideways around the trunks and limbs of lakeside trees.

Most Red-breasted Nuthatches migrate but a few stay in the area each winter. They are of course attracted to feeders and become regular visitors to feed on fat and sunflower seeds. In the autumn of some years, the bush is literally alive with nuthatches; in others only a small number will be encountered.

Nesting is carried out in a tiny cavity usually placed high in a dead tree. The entrance of the cavity is often smeared with sticky pine pitch, the purpose of which is open to speculation.

# White-breasted Nuthatch

*Sitta carolinensis*

Rare - Transient

Anytime after the first of September, a few of these nuthatches can be expected. Occasionally one will winter at a feeder and can be regularly observed. The wintering birds disappear as soon as the weather moderates in the spring.

This bird is fairly common west of Fort Frances.

## Brown Creeper

*Certhia americana*

Frequent - Summer Resident

An inconspicuous little bird, it is probably more common in Quetico than records would indicate. It prefers to inhabit mature Black Spruce and Jack Pine stands. The scaly bark of these trees harbours abundant small insects which the creeper finds and extracts with its long curved bill.

The nest is artfully concealed behind a slab of bark on the side of a dead spruce or pine and is exceedingly difficult to find. There is a definite southerly movement of creepers during September and October. Several winter records exist indicating that some Brown Creepers occasionally spend the winter in the area.

Earliest date: April 14
Latest date: December 19

## Carolina Wren

*Thryothorus ludovicianus*

Vagrant

The single record for this southern species occurred on November 15, 1990, when one came to a feeder in Atikokan. In spite of severe cold and frequent snowfalls, it was seen at the feeder from time to time until December 18, 1990.

## House Wren

*Troglodytes aedon*

Uncommon - Summer Resident

Records in Quetico for this wren are few and consist almost entirely of individuals noted during the spring and fall migratory periods.

A few pairs nest each year in birdhouses in the town of Atikokan. An early morning stroll down the residential streets in early June will quickly reveal singing males. Pairs seem to return to the same nest site each year but numbers do fluctuate from year to year.

Once the males stop singing in mid-summer, the House Wren is difficult to find. The family groups of adults and fledged young frequent brushy thickets and do not make their presence obvious.

Earliest date:  May 11
Latest date:  September 21

# Winter Wren
*Troglodytes troglodytes*

Frequent - Summer Resident

As canoeists drift slowly over the quiet mist-shrouded waters of Quetico in the early morning, a wild and beautiful bubbling song will often be heard emanating from the depths of the shoreline forest. Most will never know the identity of the singer and would be surprised to find out the originator is a tiny brown bird not much larger than a thumb.

With a little care and patience, the Winter Wren, once heard, can be observed. The bird will always see the observer first and the reward for braving a cloud of mosquitoes is often a glimpse of the bird as it disappears into a tangle of dead branches and vegetation on the forest floor. There are no records for the bird during the winter.

Earliest date:  April 11
Latest date:  September 30

# Sedge Wren
*Cistothorus platensis*

Uncommon - Summer Resident

Extensive grassy and sedge marshes, the preferred habitat of this wren, are not common in Quetico or the Atikokan area. It should be looked for at the mouth of Deux Rivieres Creek at the north end of Sturgeon Lake and can be found most years at the mouth of Caribus Creek just west of Atikokan.

Living as it does in a somewhat open habitat, it is easy to hear and generally easy to see. With a little care the nest can be located, a perfect globe of woven grasses well hidden in standing grass. In common with other wrens, several nests are built but only one is used for laying eggs.

It is a nervous little bird, never still for a moment and its habit of cocking its tail over its back is most amusing.

Earliest date:  May 15
Latest date:  July 4

## Marsh Wren

*Cistothorus palustris*

Rare - Summer Resident

Most often found in extensive stands of cattails, this interesting wren is unfortunately seldom recorded in Quetico. Cattail growth extensive enough to attract it is practically non-existent in the park. The best places to look for it are in the big marshes of Steep Rock Lake and the Auxiliary Rawn Reservoir near Atikokan.

When singing, it is easy to find and will usually approach an observer in response to "pishing". Even then a good look at the bird may be difficult to obtain as it tends to keep well hidden in the dense cattails.

Earliest date: June 9
Latest date: September 29

## Golden-crowned Kinglet
*Regulus satrapa*

Frequent - Summer Resident

Look for this tiny bird in the tree tops of mature spruce and mixed spruce and Jack Pine stands. Its high-pitched short song is usually the first indication of its presence. During the fall migration, especially in late September, this kinglet is much easier to find and observe. Slowly moving flocks of kinglets, chickadees, Red-breasted Nuthatches and Downy Woodpeckers can be encountered almost anywhere in the park.

During the mild winter of 1982-83 the first winter records for the Golden-crowned Kinglet occurred.

Earliest date: April 14
Latest date: October 19

## Ruby-crowned Kinglet
*Regulus calendula*

Common - Summer Resident

One of the most welcome of the returning spring

birds, the Ruby-crowned Kinglet announces its arrival with its song, a long and loud bubbling cascade of sound. The tiny bird is hard to see in the tops of mature conifers, its preferred breeding habitat. It lingers in the park until the first snows of late October and then is gone until the following April.

The globular nest of plant felt is placed safely and well hidden in the topmost branches of a spruce. It is usually only found by watching the adults carrying material to the site, or later, food for the young.

Earliest date: April 15
Latest date: October 12

## Eastern Bluebird

*Sialia sialis*

Uncommon - Summer Resident

Favouring more open country, bluebirds are not known to breed in the park but do so in the Atikokan area. Each year a few pairs use nesting boxes and rear their young successfully.

It is a fairly common breeding bird in the farming country west of Fort Frances.

Earliest date: April 24
Latest date: October 16

# Mountain Bluebird

*Sialia currucoides*

Vagrant

There are two records of this western species. The first was near Eva Lake, 32 km. east of Atikokan, on May 19, 1967. The bird remained in the area for two days. The second was found April 7, 1991, just north of Atikokan near Marmion Lake.

Although it prefers open country, look for it during the spring and fall migration periods.


# Veery

*Catharus fuscescens*

Frequent - Summer Resident

The Veery's distribution is scattered throughout the park and Atikokan. Birds will be found in a certain area for years in a row but will be just as consistently absent from seemingly similar habitat in surrounding areas. It is a bird of damp forest ravines and is often associated with dense alder growth along streams and small ponds.

In the town of Atikokan, the evening song of the Veery is frequently heard along the banks of the Atikokan River.

Earliest date: May 13
Latest date: September 30

# Gray-cheeked Thrush

*Catharus minimus*

Rare - Transient

The few records for this thrush have been made during the fall migration period. The only records for Quetico consist of calling birds migrating at night in late August. Its status is not clear and the difficulty in identifying it has not helped the situation. It may be more frequent during migration than the few records indicate.

All brown-coloured thrushes should be carefully observed in case they are this species.

Earliest date:  September 6
Latest date:  September 13


# Swainson's Thrush

*Catharus ustulatus*

Common - Summer Resident

This is another of the boreal forest songsters that make the early mornings and late evenings enjoyable and memorable. The Swainson's Thrush seems to favour mature forests consisting of a mixture of coniferous and deciduous trees.

The song of this thrush is similar to the Veery

except it has an upward trend rather than a downward one. During the fall migration the flight call of this thrush is frequently heard as the birds fly overhead during the night.

Earliest date:  May 2
Latest date:  October 1

## Hermit Thrush
*Catharus guttatus*

Frequent - Summer Resident

The beautiful song of the Hermit Thrush is one of the characteristic and memorable sounds of the Quetico wilderness. Listening to its flute-like melodies issuing from the lakeside forest as dusk slowly fades to darkness is a never-to-be forgotten experience.

The Hermit Thrush prefers stands of mature Black Spruce and the edges of Black Spruce bogs as breeding sites. The nest, always discovered by accident, is carefully hidden in a clump of sphagnum moss.

It is one of the last of the thrushes to leave in the fall, lingering on well past the time when the first snowfalls have occurred.

Earliest date:  April 14
Latest date:  October 19

**Hermit Thrush**

# American Robin

*Turdus migratorius*

Common - Summer Resident

Nearly everyone is familiar with the Robin, a common backyard bird throughout most of North America. The Robins in Quetico are quite different, however. In the mature forests of the park, the Robin is a shy and secretive resident, seldom permitting more than a momentary glimpse as it slips off into the shadows of the forest. Its well-known carolling song is frequently heard in the park, but the singer is difficult to observe. In contrast, they revert to their more well-known habits and are common around the yards of Atikokan residences.

The first Robins arrive in the spring as soon as the first bare patches of ground appear. They remain quite late in the fall, particularly if there is an abundant crop of mountain ash berries on which to feed. A few stay the winter, again subsisting on mountain ash berries and the fruit of ornamental crab apples.

Earliest date: March 30
Latest date: December 19

## Varied Thrush
*Ixoreus naevius*

Vagrant

A single example of this western thrush was recorded in Atikokan on September 26, 1965 with a flock of American Robins.

It is the only record for the area. All flocks of American Robins in the spring and the fall should be carefully looked over for this species.

## Gray Catbird
*Dumetella carolinensis*

Uncommon - Summer Resident

Catbirds seem to be restricted to the wooded areas along the Atikokan River in the town of Atikokan. Here, several pairs can be recorded by canoeing down the river in the early morning.

Park records are few, although the bird's secretive nature may in part account for its apparent scarcity.

Earliest date:  May 7
Latest date:  December 9

# Northern Mockingbird

*Mimus polyglottos*

Rare - Transient

Several records for this southern species have been made in Quetico and the Atikokan area.

One spent the winter in Atikokan, taking advantage of several feeders to survive temperatures of -35 degrees C. Watch for it during the spring and fall migration periods.

# Sage Thrasher

*Oreoscoptes montanus*

Vagrant

On June 3, 1987, a slim, sandy-coloured bird appeared on the lawn of the Atikokan weather station. Several observers followed the bird as it fed on the open lawns and driveways of a nearby trailer park. It was identified as a Sage Thrasher in typical worn and faded spring plumage and became the first record of the species for the area. The characteristic white wing bars were almost nonexistent but the breast spotting was clear and quite distinct.

The Sage Thrasher is a western species found in the desert and sage areas south from central British Columbia through the United States.

# Brown Thrasher

*Toxostoma rufum*

Uncommon - Summer Resident

The Brown Thrasher likes to live in open brush areas and since very little of this habitat is available in Quetico, records are almost entirely of migrating individuals.

Several pairs nest in and around the town of Atikokan, the brushy fields near the Airport being a favoured location. The males can be easily watched when they sing from the top of a tree or bush. Otherwise, this impressive reddish-brown bird hides in heavy vegetation, making observation difficult.

Elsewhere in the Atikokan area, recent cutovers that are in the early stages of regeneration should be checked for the presence of thrashers.

Earliest date: May 4
Latest date: November 10

# American Pipit

*Anthus rubescens*

Uncommon - Transient

This species is to be looked for during the spring migration period, particularly in May, and in the fall migration period, usuually in September. The best places to watch for it are along rocky or sandy beaches or on small rocky islands, as it favours sites that are closely associated with water, at least during migration.

Pipits can be very inconspicuous. They are often only noticed when they fly up from almost beneath the feet of the observer. They are interesting birds to watch as they sedately walk along with occasional dips of their white-edged tails.

Earliest date:  May 10
Latest date:  October 15

## Bohemian Waxwing

*Bombycilla garrulus*

Uncommon - Winter Visitor

This impressive bird makes its appearance in the Atikokan area well after the winter snows have covered the land.

Although occasionally noted in Mountain Ash trees throughout the area, the best place to look for them is in the town of Atikokan. They are attracted by the abundance of ornamental tree fruits and will remain until the food supply is gone.

They are irregular in their visits and may not appear at all during some winters. Occasionally, a few will remain in the area into early April but most have left by early March, returning to their subarctic breeding grounds.

Earliest date: October 4
Latest date: April 10

## Cedar Waxwing
*Bombycilla cedrorum*

Common - Summer Resident

Cedar Waxwings do not arrive in the park until late May or even early June. They are thus one of the last migrants to arrive. In the fall flocks will linger, particularly if there has been an abundant crop of wild berries, but usually all are gone by early December.

During the winter of 1982-83, several flocks appeared in the town of Atikokan and fed on Mountain Ash berries and other ornamental tree fruits for the area's first winter records.

Cedar Waxwings often sit in the tops of dead trees from which they make short flights to catch insects.

Earliest date: May 13
Latest date: November 21

# Northern Shrike
*Lanius excubitor*

Occasional - Winter Visitor

When the park is covered with snow and locked in the icy grip of winter, few birds are to be seen. Occasionally a long-tailed grayish form will be noted at the top of a tall tree. Almost always it will be a Gray Jay but each must be looked at carefully for occasionally it is a Northern Shrike. It is an aggressive bird and keeps the winter flocks of redpolls and chickadees on the alert.

Northern Shrikes move through the area southward starting in early October. One or two will usually remain in the town of Atikokan each winter, living off small birds caught at feeders.

Earliest date:  October 2
Latest date:  April 12

# Loggerhead Shrike
*Lanius ludovicianus*

Vagrant

A single bird was observed May 4, 1992 at Sawmill Bay of Apungsisagen Lake.

# European Starling
*Sturnus vulgaris*

Common - Permanent Resident

Starlings are found in scattered pairs throughout Quetico during the summer. They utilize abandoned woodpecker holes in dead trees, quite often those found standing in beaver ponds.

In the town of Atikokan they are a common bird, quite at home in the urban setting and nesting wherever a hole or loose board permits access to a nesting space. Starlings nest early with young being fed in late May. Young of the year, once on the wing, form flocks with adults and forage on lawns and other open areas throughout town.

Most starlings leave the area for the winter. Some small groups remain each year and visit feeders for food.


# Solitary Vireo
*Vireo solitarius*

Frequent - Summer Resident

This is the first of the vireos to return in the spring. The trees are just starting to leaf out in mid-May when the songs of this vireo are heard. It favours mature forest with a mixture of  coniferous and deciduous trees and is generally scattered throughout the park and the Atikokan area.

Earliest date: May 10
Latest date: September 18

## Warbling Vireo
*Vireo gilvus*

Rare - Summer Resident

This inconspicuous vireo makes up for its rather drab appearance with its beautiful warbling song. Unfortunately it is but a rare resident found only at Sandpoint Lake in the southwest corner of the Atikokan area. In Quetico, it has been recorded only as a rare migrant. It favours stands of birch or aspen as nesting sites. The Warbling Vireo is another of the birds that become quite common from Fort Frances westward.

Earliest date: May 14
Latest date: September 17

## Philadelphia Vireo
*Vireo philadelphicus*

Uncommon - Summer Resident

This vireo is likely more common in Quetico than

the few records indicate. Its song is quite similar to the Red-eyed Vireo and is probably often mistaken for this species unless the singing bird can be seen.

The Philadelphia Vireo appears to favour mature aspen stands as its summer home. The western part of Quetico has many such stands and this is the best area in the park to look for this vireo.

In late August - September, during the main fall migration period, the Philadelphia Vireo is frequently encountered in the flocks of warblers and other vireos moving slowly south.

Earliest date:  May 17
Latest date:  November 2


## Red-eyed Vireo
*Vireo olivaceus*

Common - Summer Resident

On warm days in early summer, the songs of the Red-eyed Vireo seem to come from almost every tree. It is very common throughout the park and the Atikokan area. This vireo uses a wide range of habitat from mature aspen forests to urban backyards. It is one of the last of the forest birds to stop singing in late summer and continues to do so even during migration.

Their attractive basket-like nest of woven plant fibre

and curls of birch bark are commonly found in shrubs and bushes after leaf fall.

Earliest date: May 13
Latest date: September 24

## Golden-winged Warbler
*Vermivora chrysoptera*

Vagrant

The presence of this warbler in Quetico is based on a single bird observed in the tall aspens near the Dawson Trail Campgrounds office on French Lake, June 1, 1975.

It was first noticed by park naturalist Doug Haddow when he heard its distinctive buzzy song. It apparently breeds in small numbers in the Rainy River area, 240 km. west of Quetico.

## Tennessee Warbler
*Vermivora peregrina*

Common - Summer Resident

This warbler loves thick tangles of alders and spruce in wet boggy areas. It is very easy to hear but difficult to see. To search it out, the observer must be prepared to fight mosquitoes, thick vegetation and soggy footing.

The nest is placed on the ground, usually well hidden in a sphagnum moss clump, and is difficult to find.

Earliest date:  May 13
Latest date:  October 19

## Orange-crowned Warbler
*Vermivora celata*

Uncommon - Transient

Noted in small numbers during the spring and fall migration periods, this unassuming Warbler is not known to breed in Quetico or the Atikokan area.

It is not a common bird and during migration may be encountered in almost any habitat.

Earliest date:  May 10
Latest date:  September 28

## Nashville Warbler
*Vermivora ruficapilla*

Common - Summer Resident

This Warbler is found throughout the park and the Atikokan area, and utilizes a wide range of habitats.

Generally, it prefers mixed forest of varying age interspersed with damp alder thickets and Black Spruce bogs. It is perhaps the most common warbler encountered and is also one of the first to arrive in the spring. The nest is placed on the ground well hidden in the mosses and litter of the forest floor.

Earliest date: May 3
Latest date:  October 3

## Northern Parula

*Parula americana*

Frequent - Summer Resident

Northern Parulas are found scattered throughout the park and the Atikokan area. They prefer stands of mature aspen or birch, with a scattering of conifers usually as an understory. The buzzy song is quite noticeable but the bird is difficult to see as it tends to stay high in the leafy tree tops.

There are wide gaps in its distribution.  For example, it is relatively common at French Lake in Quetico but generally absent around Atikokan.

Earliest date:  May 9
Latest date:  September 13

# Yellow Warbler

*Dendroica petechia*

Frequent - Summer Resident

Yellow Warblers are scarce in Quetico and most records are for migrants. It is occasionally found nesting in brushy clearings created by the tree-cutting activities of a beaver colony. In Atikokan, its status is quite different. It is a common backyard bird of the urban area, nesting throughout the town in ornamental shrubbery. As in the park, its numbers diminish significantly away from town.

Earliest date:  May 11
Latest date:  September 11

# Chestnut-sided Warbler

*Dendroica pensylvanica*

Common - Summer Resident

Found throughout the park and the Atikokan area, this warbler favours brushy areas such as those found in recently burned or cutover areas. It will also utilize small pockets of open areas surrounded by mature forest.

This is a warbler that has two alternate songs which can be confusing for the observer.

Earliest date:  April 30
Latest date:  September 13

# Magnolia Warbler
*Dendroica magnolia*

Common - Summer Resident

This beautiful warbler inhabits the thick coniferous understory in mature deciduous and mixed wood stands. It is a confiding bird and a singing male can be closely approached. The nest is usually placed in a small fir or spruce towards the end of a branch, well hidden by other branches overhead. Its song has a rising, questioning quality which, once heard, is easy to remember.

Earliest date:  May 13
Latest date:  September 27

# Cape May Warbler
*Dendroica tigrina*

Uncommon - Summer Resident

This warbler is clearly associated with outbreaks of Spruce Budworm. Throughout the park and the Atikokan area, large infestations of the insect occasionally occur. When this happens, Cape May Warblers can be found in the affected areas in good numbers.  In 1983 a major infestation occurred in and around the town of Atikokan. Cape Mays were correspondingly common.  Usually only one or two records during migration are made in a year. In any year, middle-aged stands of spruce and Balsam Fir should be checked for this warbler.

Earliest date: May 9
Latest date: September 13


# Black-throated Blue Warbler
*Dendroica caerulescens*

Occasional - Summer Resident

This pretty warbler is only occasionally found in Quetico and the Atikokan area. It seems to prefer stands of mature deciduous trees such as maple or aspen with a heavy deciduous understory. This type of habitat, common in the more southern hardwood forests of the province, is scarce in Quetico. Thus, the bird is likely at the northern edge of its range and thinly scattered.

Earliest date: May 16
Latest date: September 7


# Yellow-rumped Warbler
*Dendroica coronata*

Common - Summer Resident

This is the first of the migrating warblers to arrive in Quetico in the spring and the last to leave in the fall. It is also one of the most numerous migrants. In the fall it seems that every second bird in a flock of migrants is a Yellow-rumped Warbler.

For breeding, this warbler tends to prefer mature stands of Jack Pine or spruce. However, one nest in Quetico was located in a Red Pine on a small rocky island.

The male is a very pretty bird with a rather undistinguished song.

Earliest date: April 10
Latest date: October 12

## Black-throated Green Warbler
*Dendroica virens*

Frequent - Summer Resident

Look for this pretty warbler in mature stands of spruce that also contain a few scattered aspen and birch.

Its distinctive buzzy song is usually the first indication of its presence. Black-throated Green Warblers are evenly scattered throughout the park and can usually be found by looking in the appropriate habitat.

Earliest date: May 7
Latest date: September 26

## Blackburnian Warbler
*Dendroica fusca*

Common - Summer Resident

This beautifully-plumaged warbler with its flame orange throat is difficult to watch since it inhabits the very tops of trees in mature spruce and Jack Pine forests. Aspen stands with a mixture of conifer are also used.

It has two quite distinct songs and can cause the observer some anxious moments until one becomes familiar with both.

The nest is well hidden and practically inaccessible at the top of a tall spruce.

Earliest date:  May 10
Latest date:  September 26


## Pine Warbler
*Dendroica pinus*

Uncommon - Summer Resident

Look for this warbler in shoreline stands of Red Pine and White Pine, particularly in the southern portion of Quetico.  It is rare or absent in the northern parts of the Atikokan area.

The song, usually the first indication of its presence,

is quite similar to the Chipping Sparrow and the bird can accordingly be overlooked.

A pair has nested most years in the Red Pine trees around the Canada Customs station on Sand Point Lake.

Earliest date: May 10
Latest date: September 21

## Palm Warbler
*Dendroica palmarum*

Frequent - Summer Resident

Most Palm Warblers recorded in Quetico are migrants encountered in the spring and the fall. Some remain to nest and should be looked for in open Black Spruce and Tamarack bogs. Its distribution is somewhat scattered with one bog having a couple of pairs and apparently similar bogs in the vicinity not containing any.

It tends to migrate in the fall a little later than most other warblers.

Earliest date: May 2
Latest date: October 13

# Bay-breasted Warbler
*Dendroica castanea*

Uncommon - Summer Resident

Look for this large warbler in stands of mature spruce and Jack Pine. It has a very high-pitched song which can be difficult for some people to hear.

It is more common during the fall migration but care must be taken not to confuse it with the very similarly autumn-plumaged Blackpoll Warbler.

Earliest date:  May 16
Latest date:  September 15

# Blackpoll Warbler
*Dendroica striata*

Occasional - Transient

During the spring migration, all black and white warblers should be carefully checked for this species. It does not remain in the park to breed, only passing through in apparently small numbers during migration. Similar to the Bay-breasted Warbler, its high-pitched song can be difficult to hear.

Earliest date:  May 18
Latest date:  September 13

# Black-and-white Warbler

*Mniotila varia*

Common - Summer Resident

An early spring migrant, the Black-and-white Warbler is usually heard and seen before the leaves have started to emerge.

It favours mature stands of mixed coniferous and deciduous trees and is easily found throughout the park and the Atikokan area. Although it spends most of its time creeping about the trunk and higher limbs of trees, its nest is carefully hidden on the forest floor.

Earliest date:  April 24
Latest date:  September 17

# American Redstart

*Setophaga ruticilla*

Frequent - Summer Resident

Common during migration, this beautiful warbler is a rare breeder in Quetico. Elsewhere in the Atikokan area it is more frequently found, particularly along the Atikokan River.

Thick-growing alder and willow in damp areas are favoured. The impressive black, orange and white plumage of the male is not attained until the end of its second season and singing males still in the female-like plumage are occasionally encountered each spring.

Earliest date:  May 5
Latest date:  September 17

## Prothonotary Warbler
*Protonotaria citrea*

Vagrant

A single record of this impressive warbler exists for the park.  On April 26, 1976, a male of this species was found in the shoreline vegetation along the Pickerel River where it empties into French Lake.  It remained in the area for several days.  Due to its brilliant colour and the total lack of leaf cover at that early date it was easy to observe.

The closest breeding population of this species is in southeastern Minnesota.

## Ovenbird
*Seiurus aurocapillus*

Common - Summer Resident

The loud "teacher, teacher, teacher" song of this ground-dwelling warbler is a common sound of the forests of Quetico.  The Ovenbird also has a less frequently-heard flight song given as the bird rises upward beyond the tops of the forest trees and slowly descends on upraised wings. The flight song is often heard at night during early summer.

The bird is named after its nesting habits. The nest is placed on the ground and is completely covered over. Access is gained by a small hole in the side and the whole structure resembles an old-fashioned clay oven.

Earliest date:  May 6
Latest date:  September 15

## Northern Waterthrush
*Seiurus noveboracensis*

Frequent - Summer Resident

As its name implies, this large warbler is usually associated with water. It may be a back bay on a lake or a beaver pond but most commonly it seems to prefer running water found in fast-flowing streams and brooks.

In Quetico it is frequently found along the short rock-strewn waterways that connect the many lakes of the park.

It has a loud song, easily heard above the noise of rapids and small waterfalls.

Earliest date:  May 11
Latest date:  September 27

**<u>Northern Waterthrush</u>**

## Connecticut Warbler

*Oporornis agilis*

Uncommon - Summer Resident

One of the park's specialities, this warbler makes its home in open Black Spruce and Tamarack bogs. It is a shy bird and although the loud song can be heard for a long distance, obtaining a view of the bird can be difficult. It usually sings well-hidden in the thick top of a spruce or a Tamarack and is quick to leave on the approach of an incautious observer.

To date, a nest with eggs of this warbler has not been found in Ontario. It is another ground-nesting warbler and the nest is hidden deep in a clump of sphagnum moss.

Earliest date: May 22
Latest date: August 13

## Mourning Warbler

*Oporornis philadelphia*

Common - Summer Resident

The Mourning Warbler frequents brushy tangles such as those found along the edges of beaver ponds and in recent burns or cutovers. It is somewhat secretive and although its song attracts attention, seeing it can be a little difficult.

It is found throughout the park and the Atikokan area, but avoids extensive stands of mature trees.

Earliest date:  May 18
Latest date:  September 16

Mourning Warbler

# Common Yellowthroat
*Geothlypis trichas*

Common - Summer Resident

This distinctively-marked warbler is found throughout Quetico wherever marshy and somewhat open conditions occur. Old, partly grown-over abandoned beaver ponds, the edges of slow-moving streams and, where they occur, extensive cattail marshes are all favoured habitats.

It is a curious bird and can be coaxed out of hiding in a vegetation tangle by "pishing". The bright yellow underparts and the contrasting black mask of the adult male can then be noted.

The nest is placed in a tussock of grass or other thick vegetation, often surrounded by water.

Earliest date: May 15
Latest date: September 6

# Wilson's Warbler
*Wilsonia pusilla*

Uncommon - Summer Resident

Look for this warbler along the edges of lakes or streams that are bordered by an extensive growth of willow. This habitat is scarce in Quetico, but is common along the Atikokan River from the town of Atikokan to the river mouth in Lower Steep Rock Lake. During migration it is usually noted in the company of other warblers.

Earliest date: May 15
Latest date: September 14

## Canada Warbler

*Wilsonia canadensis*

Frequent - Summer Resident

This warbler frequents a variety of habitats but seems to favour brushy, semi-open hillsides, such as those found around the edges of beaver ponds. By cutting the larger trees, the beavers create openings that are rapidly overgrown with hazel, aspen, birch and Balsam Fir. In these tangles, the Canada Warbler lives and nests. It has a somewhat emphatic song which attracts attention. However, the singer is not inclined to leave the security of thick vegetation and can be difficult to observe.

Earliest date: May 17
Latest date: September 7

# Scarlet Tanager
*Piranga olivacea*

Uncommon - Summer Resident

Look for this intensely-coloured bird in areas of mature mixed forest. It is not common in Quetico but can be found throughout with a little effort. Listen for its song which is Robin-like with an overall burry or buzzy quality.

Tanagers arrive in the spring just as the trees are covered with newly-grown leaves. The males immediately announce their presence by singing from the tops of the tallest trees in their territory. Most have left the park by the first of September.

Earliest date: May 16
Latest date: October 3

# Summer Tanager
*Piranga rubra*

Vagrant

On May 13, 1982, five tanagers were noticed at a feeder in the town of Atikokan. One of them was photographed and subsequently identified as a male Summer Tanager, just changing into breeding plumage. On October 20, 1992, a brilliant male was noted at an Atikokan feeder and remained in the area for several days, in spite of snow and cold temperatures.

# Northern Cardinal

*Cardinalis cardinalis*

Vagrant

The first area record for this species was made on November 6, 1981, in Atikokan. A male cardinal visited a feeder for two days and then was not seen again. During the winter of 1990 - 91, a female was seen at several Atikokan feeders.

# Rose-breasted Grosbeak

*Pheucticus ludovicianus*

Frequent - Summer Resident

The warbling, robin-like song of this impressively-marked grosbeak is the first indication of its springtime return in mid-May. It frequents a wide variety of habitat but favours mature and semi-mature forests of mixed coniferous and deciduous trees. Openings in the forest, such as the edges of beaver ponds where the brush is heavy and surrounded by large trees, are especially attractive. The males lose their brilliant plumage in late summer and resemble the immatures and females during fall migration. Most have left the park and the area by mid-September.

Earliest date:  May 13
Latest date:  October 23

# Indigo Bunting

*Passerina cyanea*

Uncommon - Summer Resident

The Indigo Bunting appears to be just on the edge of its northern range in Quetico.  Look for it in brushy areas around old beaver ponds and in burns or old logging areas.

In the rest of the Atikokan area, the edges of abandoned gravel pits are favoured locations as is the area around the Atikokan airport.

The male sings from a conspicuous perch at the top of a tree but can be hard to see in spite of its blue plumage.

Earliest date:  May 26
Latest date:  November 5

# Rufous-sided Towhee

*Pipilo erythrophthalmus*

Rare - Transient

There are four records for this handsome bird in Quetico and Atikokan.  One visited, for several days, the island on which the Cache Bay Ranger Station is located.  The second bird was noted in the park interior on Kahshahpiwi Lake.  The third record was a male of the "western" or "spotted" subspecies that regularly visited a feeder in Atikokan for some time and was first noted on October 27, 1984. A fourth male of the "eastern" subspecies was present in Atikokan for several days around November 10, 1991.


## American Tree Sparrow
*Spizella arborea*

Common - Transient

Tree Sparrows pass through Quetico and the Atikokan area in considerable numbers each spring and fall. They do not form large flocks and usually several well-scattered individuals are encountered. They prefer brushy, semi-open areas such as the edges of beaver ponds, cutovers or burned areas.

There are only two winter records. These were of birds that frequented feeders in Atikokan during the winters of 1979 and 1980.

Earliest date:  September 27
Latest date:  April 16

# Chipping Sparrow

*Spizella passerina*

Common - Summer Resident

This small sparrow is found throughout Quetico and the Atikokan area. The first migrants arrive in early May and the males advertise their presence by singing from an open elevated perch.

In Quetico, Chipping Sparrows frequent a wide variety of habitats from mature coniferous forest to recent burns. In Atikokan, it is a common bird of the residential area, nesting in bushes and shrubs, often close to houses.

Earliest date:  April 21
Latest date:  November 2

# Clay-colored Sparrow

*Spizella pallida*

Occasional - Summer Resident

This grayish sparrow with the strange buzzy song is rarely encountered in Quetico. Its habitat preference appears to be semi-open areas with a good scattering of bushes and shrubs. In Atikokan, it is most frequently found near the airport and along the Atikokan River. It is another western species that becomes common west of Fort Frances.

Earliest date:  May 18
Latest date:  September 15

# Vesper Sparrow

*Pooecetes gramineus*

Uncommon - Summer Resident

This large sparrow is only found in the Atikokan area around the town airport. Several pairs nest each year in the grassy brushy areas that surround the landing strip.

In Quetico, it has been recorded only rarely as a visitor during the spring and fall migration periods.

Earliest date:  April 21
Latest date:  October 5

# Savannah Sparrow

*Passerculus sandwichensis*

Frequent - Summer Resident

Because of a lack of open areas, the Savannah Sparrow is uncommon in Quetico. A few pair remain in the park each summer to nest in the old grass-covered beaver meadows and in short grass marshes. During migration, they can be expected anywhere particularly along wide beaches and shorelines. In the rest of the Atikokan area, they are found in any open space that provides grassy cover. Many nest in and around Atikokan in weedy lots and fields. Other favoured locations include the Flanders area and Atikokan Airport. During late

September and early October  Savannah Sparrows can be found in the flocks of migrants that pass through the area. Many of these are dark, heavily-streaked individuals, quite different in colour than the breeding birds.

Earliest date:  April 21
Latest date:  September 30

## Lark Sparrow
*Chondestes grammacus*

Vagrant

On May 21, 1966, Peruniak observed a Lark Sparrow at the old farm near the Hardy Dam just east of Atikokan.  A second bird was recorded on May 5, 1985, along the Canadian National Railway west of Atikokan at Caribus Creek and a third was noted April 16, 1986, also near the Hardy Dam.

## Le Conte's Sparrow
*Ammodramus leconteii*

Occasional - Summer Resident

A difficult sparrow to see and identify, it is even more difficult to find.  It prefers a breeding habitat of wet grassy and  weedy fields or short grass marshes,  both of which are very scarce in Quetico. In 1983, two singing males could regularly be found in the grassy flats at the south end of French Lake.

Elsewhere in the Atikokan area, the only constant place Le Conte's Sparrow can be found is in the short grass marsh at the mouth of Caribus Creek on Apungsisagen Lake. Several pairs nest there each year. The song is similar to that of the Savannah Sparrow but is even more insect-like and difficult to hear.

Earliest date:  May 15
Latest date:  June 27

## Fox Sparrow
*Passerella iliaca*

Frequent - Transient

This large richly-coloured sparrow visits the park during migration in both the spring and the fall. It is rather shy and obtaining a good view of it can be difficult as it tends to stay in heavy brushy cover. Usually it is seen as a flash of rusty red as it flies from the edge of a trail or portage into the bush.

Earliest date:  April 7
Latest date:  November 25

# Song Sparrow
*Melospiza melodia*

Common - Summer Resident

The Song Sparrow is found throughout Quetico and the Atikokan area. It prefers brushy areas in association with water and is most likely to be found along the edges of lakes, streams and beaver ponds.

It is an early migrant and is often back before the ice leaves the lakes. This does not stop the males from singing and their beautiful notes are a welcome sound after the silences of winter.

Earliest date:  March 25
Latest date:  September 25


# Lincoln's Sparrow
*Melospiza lincolnii*

Frequent - Summer Resident

Look for this secretive sparrow in Black Spruce and Tamarack bogs. Singing males are easy to locate and with care, a good view can be obtained.

During migration it can be expected almost anywhere but is extremely shy and retiring.

It is another resident of the bogs, nesting in the dense mats of sphagnum moss that cover the ground. The nest is very difficult to locate.

Earliest date:  April 30
Latest date:  October 18

Lincoln's Sparrow

# Swamp Sparrow

*Melospiza georgiana*

Common - Summer Resident

Swamp Sparrows, as their name implies, can be found wherever swampy or marshy conditions occur in Quetico. This could be a stand of cattails or the brushy areas along creeks and streams. Its song is easily heard but the songster may be difficult to see.

Often all that is glimpsed is a brownish long-tailed bird that suddenly rises out of the vegetation and just as quickly disappears.

Earliest date: April 22
Latest date: September 25

# White-throated Sparrow

*Zonotrichia albicollis*

Common - Summer Resident

Found throughout Quetico and the Atikokan area, the White-throat is heard by every canoeist in Quetico. Its clear "Sweet Canada Canada Canada" song is easily recognized and remembered although it may be a little difficult to obtain a good view of the singer.

The first White-throats arrive in the spring in late

April and immediately establish a nesting territory. The young of the year are usually out of the nest by mid-July and the family groups remain together until fall migration begins in late September. Large flocks of White-throats and other sparrows are then found everywhere throughout the park.

There are several winter records of birds at feeders in the town of Atikokan and the surrounding area.

Earliest date:  April 23
Latest date:  October 20


# White-crowned Sparrow
*Zonotrichia leucophrys*

Common - Transient

This sparrow is only recorded in the park during the spring and fall migration period. Movement is rapid in the spring and the birds are soon gone northward to their breeding areas. In the fall, movement is more leisurely and large flocks of the black and white-headed adults and brown birds of the year are encountered everywhere. The males occasionally give their beautiful song while on migration.

Earliest date:  April 30
Latest date:  October 16

# Harris' Sparrow
*Zonotrichia querula*

Frequent - Transient

Look for this impressive sparrow among the migrating flocks of White-throated Sparrows and White-crowned Sparrows that pass through Quetico in great numbers each spring and fall.

In the spring the black head, face and chest of the adults are unmistakable. . Fall birds and immatures have considerably less black in the plumage but still retain enough for easy identification.

They do not remain long in spring but tend to move with less urgency in the fall. Several will remain around active feeders for many days in late September and early October.

Earliest date: May 9
Latest date: October 14

# Dark-eyed Junco
*Junco hyemalis*

Frequent - Summer Resident

During the spring and fall migration periods, large numbers of juncos pass through Quetico and the Atikokan area. Some remain to breed and select as nesting sites Black Spruce bogs and mixed spruce and Jack Pine stands.

The song of the male is similar to the Chipping Sparrow and is usually given from a perch midway up a tree.

Occasionally, juncos remain in the Atikokan area during the winter, staying in the vicinity of a regularly maintained feeder.

Earliest date:  April 2
Latest date:  October 30

## Lapland Longspur
*Calcarius lapponicus*

Frequent - Transient

Flocks of longspurs move through Quetico and the Atikokan area each spring and fall. They prefer open areas, and with the general abundance of this kind of habitat in Quetico, are usually found along beaches and shorelines. They blend in perfectly with their surroundings and often are only seen when the flock flushes from almost under the observers' feet.

Elsewhere in the Atikokan area, cutovers, roadsides and gravel pits are favourite feeding and nesting areas.

Earliest date:  April 16
Latest date:  November 29

# Snow Bunting

*Plectrophenax nivalis*

Common - Transient

Large flocks of migrating Snow Buntings can be found in Quetico and the Atikokan area early each spring and late each fall. The birds frequent shorelines and beaches, the closest the park provides to their preferred open habitat.

Cutovers, gravel pits and roads are also visited and are often the best place to look for this species.

There are only two winter records; that of a small flock that stayed in the rail yards of Atikokan, apparently feeding on spilled grain, and another flock observed January 1, 1987 at the Ontario Hydro Atikokan Generating Station ash disposal site.

Earliest date: September 14
Latest date: May 17

# Bobolink

*Dolichonyx oryzivorus*

Rare - Summer Resident

One or two Bobolinks are usually recorded in the park and the Atikokan area each year during migration. Since there is an almost complete absence of open fields in Quetico, the bird's preferred habitat, it is actually of accidental occurrence in the park.

In Atikokan there are several open fields and some years a pair of migrants find these and stay for the summer. The most productive sites are Legion Point behind the Log Cabin Museum and the fields near the Ministry of Natural Resources office.

The old fields at Flanders Station, 40 km. west of Atikokan, also usually contain a pair or two.

Earliest date:  May 14
Latest date:  September 17


## Red-winged Blackbird

*Agelaius phoeniceus*

Common - Summer Resident

The Red-winged Blackbird is found everywhere in the park and the Atikokan area wherever marshy conditions exist. This may include cattail stands, grassy marshes and even open boggy areas covered in Leatherleaf. Cattails are favoured over all else.

Each winter a few of these blackbirds spend the winter in Atikokan at feeders. They do not seem to be adversely affected by intense cold as long as they can obtain sufficient food.

Earliest date:  March 29
Latest date:  November 23

**Red-Winged Blackbird**

# Eastern Meadowlark

*Sturnella magna*

Vagrant

Only one record for Quetico and the Atikokan area exists for this species. A single bird was present at French Lake for several days having first appeared on October 24, 1991.

# Western Meadowlark

*Sturnella neglecta*

Rare - Transient

This open-country bird is usually recorded in the Atikokan district each spring and is considered a vagrant from the open farming country west of Fort Frances.

The few records for Quetico include one on the staffhouse lawn at French Lake and a particularly strange one, at the Cache Bay Ranger Station, a small rocky pine-clad island in Saganaga Lake.

The few open areas in Atikokan are the places to watch and listen for this visitor in the spring.

Earliest date: March 28
Latest date: July 10

# Yellow-headed Blackbird

*Xanthocephalus xanthocephalus*

Rare - Summer Resident

This spectacular blackbird of the western prairie sloughs is only an occasional spring transient in Quetico. The large marshy bays in Lac la Croix such as Rice Bay should be checked for it by park visitors in that area.

An active colony of Yellow-headed Blackbirds has nested in the cattail marshes of the southwest arm of Steep Rock Lake for many years. Co-existing with the more numerous Red-wing Blackbirds, the Yellow-heads lay eggs just as the Red-wing young are leaving the nest. Thus little competition occurs between the two species. The nest is a woven basket of cattail leaves and grass supported by the dead cattail stems of the previous year. The nest is constructed of wet material which dries into an exceptionally strong and durable structure. It is significantly larger and deeper than the nest of the Red-wing.

In the early spring, the large flocks of migrating blackbirds should be carefully scanned for this species.

Earliest date:  April 19
Latest date:  June 10

# Rusty Blackbird

*Euphagus carolinus*

Frequent - Transient

Rare - Summer Resident

The Rusty Blackbird passes through Quetico and the Atikokan area during the spring and fall migration periods. It is found singly, in small flocks or as a component of the large flocks of Red-wings, Common Grackles and Brown-headed Cowbirds.

A few pairs remain in the area each summer and may breed although no nest has yet been found. Canoeists should observe carefully any Rusty Blackbirds encountered during the breeding season for indications of nesting.

During fall migration, birds can still be encountered in late October usually in open wet areas in burns or cutovers.

Earliest date: March 31
Latest date: January 1

# Brewer's Blackbird

*Euphagus cyanocephalus*

Uncommon - Summer Resident

Another western blackbird, it is only infrequently encountered in Quetico as a migrant. It is easy to confuse with the Rusty Blackbird and care should be taken to separate the two. Elsewhere in the Atikokan area, active nesting colonies can be found each year along the Atikokan River in Atikokan, in the grass marshes at the mouth of the Atikokan River and around the Sapawe area.

The males with their glossy black plumage and startlingly white eyes attract attention and fly out to investigate any intruder approaching the nesting colony. Nests are placed on the ground, well hidden in the vegetation.

Earliest date: April 22
Latest date: September 24

## Great-tailed Grackle
*Quiscalus mexicanus*

Accidental

On October 7, 1987, a female of this species was noted in a residential backyard in Atikokan, feeding with a flock of Common Grackles, Red-winged Blackbirds and Rusty Blackbirds. The bird was present until October 25 and was not seen again. The Great-tailed Grackle is normally found in the southwestern United States, in Texas, Arizona, New Mexico and Oklahoma. The species appears to be expanding its breeding range northward and has recently bred in Nebraska.

This record was the first occurrence of the species in Ontario.

## Common Grackle

*Quiscalus quiscula*

Common - Summer Resident

This large familiar blackbird is found throughout Quetico. Usually they are encountered as single pairs nesting near small beaver ponds. In Atikokan, it nests in conifers in residential yards and is a common bird of the town. A small colony has nested in a cattail stand in Steep Rock Lake for several years, a somewhat unusual situation.

A few grackles remain in Atikokan all winter, helped along no doubt by the presence of numerous bird feeders.

Earliest date: April 1
Latest date: November 18


## Brown-headed Cowbird

*Molothrus ater*

Frequent - Summer Resident

The cowbird is not common in Quetico, probably due to the lack of open country it prefers. Thus it is usually encountered in the park during migration. In Atikokan it is fairly common and can be found throughout the town in small flocks, feeding on lawns and other grassy areas.

On arrival in the spring, they are quick to use feeders and will return repeatedly to glean the accumulated food that has built up around the base of the feeder during the winter.

Although fledged young of the year have been observed, cowbird eggs, which are laid in the nest of other species, have not been found to date.

Earliest date:  March 30
Latest date:  October 12

# Northern Oriole

*Icterus galbula*

Rare - Summer Resident

Records for this species in Quetico and the Atikokan area consist almost entirely of vagrant birds encountered during the spring migration period.  The only known location where it breeds is in the southwest corner of the area near Sand Point Lake.  Here it exists with other area rarities such as Purple Martins and Warbling Vireos.

Earliest date:  May 18
Latest date:  July 10

## Pine Grosbeak
*Pinicola enucleator*

Common - Winter Visitor

This beautiful winter finch usually arrives in Quetico and the Atikokan area in mid-October and remains in varying numbers until mid-March. In Quetico their cheery calls are one of the few sounds that break the winter silence.

Pine Grosbeaks quickly learn to visit feeders in Atikokan and feed on sunflower seeds. The seeds of ash and Manitoba Maple trees are also favoured and flocks will remain until the trees are stripped of seeds. The birds are frequently seen along the edges of roads and highways in the area, apparently eating salt or sand.

Several hundred have been banded in Atikokan and analysis of returns indicates a two year cycle of relative abundance. The only returns have been of birds recaptured two years after banding. There are no summer records for this species.

Earliest date: October 9
Latest date: April 6

## House Finch
*Carpodacus mexicanus*

Vagrant

On October 9, 1991, a single male House Finch

visited a feeder at French Lake in Quetico and became the first record of this species for the area. Formerly a western species solely, it was introduced to the eastern United States and has spread to Southern Ontario, where it is now common.

## Purple Finch

*Carpodacus purpureus*

Common - Permanent Resident

The Purple Finch is found throughout Quetico although its numbers vary from year to year and also from season to season. It may be completely absent during some winters and abundant the next.

The beautiful warbling song of the males is heard from mid-March through the summer and is usually given from a high perch.

The Purple Finch is a wanderer and banding recapture records for the Atikokan area include birds banded in Missouri.

Each spring large numbers build up during April, frequenting feeders in Atikokan. The numbers fall off towards May and only the breeding birds remain for the summer.

# Red Crossbill

*Loxia curvirostra*

Occasional - Permanent Resident

A bird of unpredictable wanderings, the Red Crossbill may be encountered at anytime in Quetico. Flocks seem to prefer Red Pine as a food source, the birds resembling small parrots as they cling sideways and upside down to the cones as they extract the seeds. During the winter, the best place to look for this crossbill is along the edges of roads and highways. Small flocks gather on the roadsides apparently to eat salt or sand.

# White-winged Crossbill

*Loxia leucoptera*

Occasional - Permanent Resident

This crossbill is perhaps more likely to be encountered than the preceding species. It is equally unpredictable in its appearances and tends to prefer the seeds of spruce and Tamarack as food. It is also fond of salt and sand and is often seen along roadsides in winter.

# Common Redpoll
*Carduelis flammea*

Common - Winter Visitor

A winter visitor to Quetico and the Atikokan area, the Common Redpoll is another finch whose numbers vary greatly from year to year. In a good redpoll winter, large flocks are encountered everywhere, feeding on the seeds of alder and birch. In poor seed years, scarcely a one can be found.

Flocks quickly find feeders and once this food source has been located, the number of birds in the visiting flock increases steadily. Redpolls have usually left the area by late March.

Earliest date: October 19
Latest date: May 4


# Hoary Redpoll
*Carduelis hornemanni*

Rare - Winter Visitor

Look for this whitish redpoll in the flocks of Common Redpolls that visit the park each winter in varying numbers. Very light-coloured individuals can be quickly picked out of a flock; others, less well-marked, must be carefully observed before their identity is apparent. Similar to the Common Redpoll, this species is usually more likely to be seen every second winter.

# Pine Siskin

*Carduelis pinus*

Frequent - Permanent Resident

Siskins can be expected anywhere at anytime of the year. They are even more erratic and unpredictable in their numbers than the other "winter finches". Flocks wander widely and often appear to be flying around with no apparent purpose. A feeding flock will suddenly leap into the air with much calling, wheel around for a moment or two and then return to feed silently from the very tree they left a short time before.

# American Goldfinch

*Carduelis tristis*

Frequent - Summer Resident

In Quetico, goldfinches are summer birds. The first spring migrants return to the park in May with the characteristic flight call of the male being the first indication of their presence.

Nesting does not occur until quite late in the summer after thistles have bloomed and turned to seed. This food source is then used to feed the young.

Goldfinches can be encountered almost anywhere in the park, but show a preference for open areas and forest edges. During the mild 1982-83 winter, the first winter records for the goldfinch in the Atikokan area occurred. Several birds were regular visitors to feeders.

Earliest date: May 15
Latest date: October 5

## Evening Grosbeak

*Coccothraustes vespertinus*

Common - Permanent Resident

This grosbeak is noted for the unpredictability of its presence in the park from year to year and from season to season. In some years it is very common all year and in others, absent for most of the year, only to appear in numbers unexpectedly. It is a great wanderer and banded birds from Atikokan have been recovered from Vermont, New York, Michigan, Manitoba and several points in southern Ontario. In most winters, it is a frequent visitor to the feeders in town and the surrounding area. The keys on Manitoba Maple are also eaten in quantity.

The Evening Grosbeak can be expected anywhere in the park at anytime of the year.

# Brambling

*Fringilla montifringilla*

Vagrant

On October 23, 1983, a male Brambling in winter plumage was observed at the residence of the author in Atikokan. The bird was subsequently photographed and seen by many observers. It remained in the area for three days. It fed on the ground in the company of Fox Sparrows, Dark-eyed Juncos, Tree Sparrows and Purple Finches.

The normal breeding range of the Brambling is northern Europe. The presence of the bird constituted the second record for the province of Ontario. Incredibly, a second Brambling was at a feeder in Atikokan from October 4 to 7, 1991 and became the fourth provincial record.

# House Sparrow

*Passer domesticus*

Uncommon - Resident

Seeing a House Sparrow in Quetico is indeed an accomplishment. They are rarely found. Except in the town of Atikokan they are seldom seen. In Atikokan, they nest side by side with Tree Swallows in nest boxes erected in local backyards.

The House Sparrow stays for the winter but the numbers vary from year to year. Winters with prolonged cold spells appear to significantly reduce the local population and it takes a year or two of good conditions for them to recover.

Feeders operated all winter help the birds to survive.

# APPENDIX I

# A Checklist of

# the Birds of Quetico Provincial Park

# and the

# Atikokan Area

## CHECKLIST OF THE BIRDS OF QUETICO PARK AND THE ATIKOKAN AREA

C = Common   U = Uncommon   R = Rare   V = Vagrant

| SPECIES | DATE | | | | | | | | | |
|---|---|---|---|---|---|---|---|---|---|---|
| COMMON LOON – C | | | | | | | | | | |
| PIED-BILLED GREBE – C | | | | | | | | | | |
| HORNED GREBE – U | | | | | | | | | | |
| RED-NECKED GREBE – R | | | | | | | | | | |
| WESTERN GREBE – V | | | | | | | | | | |
| AMERICAN WHITE PELICAN – V | | | | | | | | | | |
| DOUBLE-CRESTED CORMORANT – U | | | | | | | | | | |
| AMERICAN BITTERN – C | | | | | | | | | | |
| LEAST BITTERN – V | | | | | | | | | | |
| GREAT BLUE HERON – C | | | | | | | | | | |
| GREAT EGRET – V | | | | | | | | | | |
| TUNDRA SWAN – U | | | | | | | | | | |
| SNOW GOOSE – U | | | | | | | | | | |
| CANADA GOOSE – C | | | | | | | | | | |
| WOOD DUCK – U | | | | | | | | | | |
| GREEN-WINGED TEAL – C | | | | | | | | | | |
| AMERICAN BLACK DUCK – C | | | | | | | | | | |
| MALLARD – C | | | | | | | | | | |
| NORTHERN PINTAIL – U | | | | | | | | | | |
| BLUE-WINGED TEAL – C | | | | | | | | | | |
| NORTHERN SHOVELER – R | | | | | | | | | | |
| GADWALL – V | | | | | | | | | | |
| AMERICAN WIGEON – C | | | | | | | | | | |
| CANVASBACK – R | | | | | | | | | | |
| REDHEAD – R | | | | | | | | | | |
| RING-NECKED DUCK – C | | | | | | | | | | |
| GREATER SCAUP – U | | | | | | | | | | |
| LESSER SCAUP – C | | | | | | | | | | |
| HARLEQUIN DUCK – V | | | | | | | | | | |
| OLDSQUAW – V | | | | | | | | | | |
| BLACK SCOTER – V | | | | | | | | | | |

## CHECKLIST OF THE BIRDS OF QUETICO PARK AND THE ATIKOKAN AREA

C = Common    U = Uncommon    R = Rare    V = Vagrant

| SPECIES | DATE | | | | | | | | |
|---|---|---|---|---|---|---|---|---|---|
| WHITE-WINGED SCOTER – R | | | | | | | | | |
| COMMON GOLDENEYE – C | | | | | | | | | |
| BUFFLEHEAD – U | | | | | | | | | |
| HOODED MERGANSER – C | | | | | | | | | |
| COMMON MERGANSER – C | | | | | | | | | |
| RED-BREASTED MERGANSER – U | | | | | | | | | |
| TURKEY VULTURE – C | | | | | | | | | |
| OSPREY – U | | | | | | | | | |
| BALD EAGLE – C | | | | | | | | | |
| NORTHERN HARRIER – U | | | | | | | | | |
| SHARP-SHINNED HAWK – C | | | | | | | | | |
| COOPER'S HAWK – R | | | | | | | | | |
| NORTHERN GOSHAWK – R | | | | | | | | | |
| RED-SHOULDERED HAWK – V | | | | | | | | | |
| BROAD-WINGED HAWK – C | | | | | | | | | |
| SWAINSON'S HAWK – V | | | | | | | | | |
| RED-TAILED HAWK – C | | | | | | | | | |
| ROUGH-LEGGED HAWK – U | | | | | | | | | |
| GOLDEN EAGLE – R | | | | | | | | | |
| AMERICAN KESTREL – C | | | | | | | | | |
| MERLIN – U | | | | | | | | | |
| PEREGRINE FALCON – R | | | | | | | | | |
| SPRUCE GROUSE – C | | | | | | | | | |
| RUFFED GROUSE – C | | | | | | | | | |
| SHARP-TAILED GROUSE – R | | | | | | | | | |
| YELLOW RAIL – R | | | | | | | | | |
| VIRGINIA RAIL – R | | | | | | | | | |
| SORA – C | | | | | | | | | |
| AMERICAN COOT – U | | | | | | | | | |
| SANDHILL CRANE – R | | | | | | | | | |
| BLACK-BELLIED PLOVER – U | | | | | | | | | |

| CHECKLIST OF THE BIRDS OF QUETICO PARK AND THE ATIKOKAN AREA | | | | | | | | | | |
|---|---|---|---|---|---|---|---|---|---|---|
| C = Common      U = Uncommon      R = Rare      V = Vagrant | | | | | | | | | | |
| SPECIES | DATE | | | | | | | | | |
| LESSER GOLDEN-PLOVER - U | | | | | | | | | | |
| SEMIPALMATED PLOVER - U | | | | | | | | | | |
| PIPING PLOVER - V | | | | | | | | | | |
| KILLDEER - C | | | | | | | | | | |
| GREATER YELLOWLEGS - U | | | | | | | | | | |
| LESSER YELLOWLEGS - U | | | | | | | | | | |
| SOLITARY SANDPIPER - U | | | | | | | | | | |
| WILLET - V | | | | | | | | | | |
| SPOTTED SANDPIPER - C | | | | | | | | | | |
| UPLAND SANDPIPER - V | | | | | | | | | | |
| WHIMBREL - V | | | | | | | | | | |
| HUDSONIAN GODWIT - V | | | | | | | | | | |
| RUDDY TURNSTONE - R | | | | | | | | | | |
| RED KNOT - R | | | | | | | | | | |
| SANDERLING - U | | | | | | | | | | |
| SEMIPALMATED SANDPIPER - U | | | | | | | | | | |
| LEAST SANDPIPER - U | | | | | | | | | | |
| WHITE-RUMPED SANDPIPER - R | | | | | | | | | | |
| BAIRD'S SANDPIPER - U | | | | | | | | | | |
| PECTORAL SANDPIPER - U | | | | | | | | | | |
| DUNLIN - R | | | | | | | | | | |
| STILT SANDPIPER - R | | | | | | | | | | |
| BUFF-BREASTED SANDPIPER - R | | | | | | | | | | |
| SHORT-BILLED DOWITCHER - U | | | | | | | | | | |
| COMMON SNIPE - C | | | | | | | | | | |
| AMERICAN WOODCOCK - C | | | | | | | | | | |
| WILSON'S PHALAROPE - R | | | | | | | | | | |
| RED-NECKED PHALAROPE - R | | | | | | | | | | |
| PARASITIC JAEGER - V | | | | | | | | | | |
| BONAPARTE'S GULL - U | | | | | | | | | | |
| GLAUCOUS GULL - V | | | | | | | | | | |

## CHECKLIST OF THE BIRDS OF QUETICO PARK AND THE ATIKOKAN AREA

C = Common        U = Uncommon        R = Rare        V = Vagrant

| SPECIES | DATE | | | | | | | | |
|---|---|---|---|---|---|---|---|---|---|
| RING-BILLED GULL - U | | | | | | | | | |
| HERRING GULL - C | | | | | | | | | |
| CASPIAN TERN - V | | | | | | | | | |
| COMMON TERN - U | | | | | | | | | |
| FORSTER'S TERN - V | | | | | | | | | |
| BLACK TERN - U | | | | | | | | | |
| MOURNING DOVE - U | | | | | | | | | |
| INCA DOVE - V | | | | | | | | | |
| BLACK-BILLED CUCKOO - U | | | | | | | | | |
| YELLOW-BILLED CUCKOO - V | | | | | | | | | |
| EASTERN SCREECH-OWL - V | | | | | | | | | |
| GREAT-HORNED OWL - U | | | | | | | | | |
| SNOWY OWL - R | | | | | | | | | |
| NORTHERN HAWK OWL - R | | | | | | | | | |
| BARRED OWL - C | | | | | | | | | |
| GREAT GRAY OWL - R | | | | | | | | | |
| LONG-EARED OWL - R | | | | | | | | | |
| SHORT-EARED OWL - R | | | | | | | | | |
| BOREAL OWL - R | | | | | | | | | |
| NORTHERN SAW-WHET OWL - U | | | | | | | | | |
| COMMON NIGHTHAWK - C | | | | | | | | | |
| WHIP-POOR-WILL - R | | | | | | | | | |
| CHIMNEY SWIFT - U | | | | | | | | | |
| RUBY-THROATED HUMMINGBIRD - C | | | | | | | | | |
| RUFOUS HUMMINGBIRD - V | | | | | | | | | |
| BELTED KINGFISHER - C | | | | | | | | | |
| RED-HEADED WOODPECKER - V | | | | | | | | | |
| YELLOW-BELLIED SAPSUCKER - C | | | | | | | | | |
| DOWNY WOODPECKER - C | | | | | | | | | |
| HAIRY WOODPECKER - C | | | | | | | | | |
| THREE-TOED WOODPECKER - R | | | | | | | | | |

## CHECKLIST OF THE BIRDS OF QUETICO PARK AND THE ATIKOKAN AREA

C = Common    U = Uncommon    R = Rare    V = Vagrant

| SPECIES | DATE | | | | | | | | | |
|---|---|---|---|---|---|---|---|---|---|---|
| BLACK-BACKED WOODPECKER – U | | | | | | | | | | |
| NORTHERN FLICKER – C | | | | | | | | | | |
| PILEATED WOODPECKER – C | | | | | | | | | | |
| OLIVE-SIDED FLYCATCHER – U | | | | | | | | | | |
| EASTERN WOOD-PEWEE – U | | | | | | | | | | |
| YELLOW-BELLIED FLYCATCHER – U | | | | | | | | | | |
| ALDER FLYCATCHER – C | | | | | | | | | | |
| LEAST FLYCATCHER – C | | | | | | | | | | |
| EASTERN PHOEBE – U | | | | | | | | | | |
| SAY'S PHOEBE – V | | | | | | | | | | |
| GREAT CRESTED FLYCATCHER – R | | | | | | | | | | |
| EASTERN KINGBIRD – C | | | | | | | | | | |
| HORNED LARK – U | | | | | | | | | | |
| PURPLE MARTIN – R | | | | | | | | | | |
| TREE SWALLOW – C | | | | | | | | | | |
| NORTHERN ROUGH-WINGED SWALLOW–C | | | | | | | | | | |
| BANK SWALLOW – U | | | | | | | | | | |
| CLIFF SWALLOW – C | | | | | | | | | | |
| BARN SWALLOW – C | | | | | | | | | | |
| GRAY JAY – C | | | | | | | | | | |
| BLUE JAY – C | | | | | | | | | | |
| BLACK-BILLED MAGPIE – R | | | | | | | | | | |
| AMERICAN CROW – C | | | | | | | | | | |
| COMMON RAVEN – C | | | | | | | | | | |
| BLACK-CAPPED CHICKADEE – C | | | | | | | | | | |
| BOREAL CHICKADEE – U | | | | | | | | | | |
| RED-BREASTED NUTHATCH – C | | | | | | | | | | |
| WHITE-BREASTED NUTHATCH – R | | | | | | | | | | |
| BROWN CREEPER – U | | | | | | | | | | |
| CAROLINA WREN – V | | | | | | | | | | |
| HOUSE WREN – U | | | | | | | | | | |

| CHECKLIST OF THE BIRDS OF QUETICO PARK AND THE ATIKOKAN AREA | | | | | | | | | |
|---|---|---|---|---|---|---|---|---|---|
| C = Common     U = Uncommon     R = Rare     V = Vagrant | | | | | | | | | |
| **SPECIES** | **DATE** | | | | | | | | |
| WINTER WREN – C | | | | | | | | | |
| SEDGE WREN – U | | | | | | | | | |
| MARSH WREN – R | | | | | | | | | |
| GOLDEN-CROWNED KINGLET – C | | | | | | | | | |
| RUBY-CROWNED KINGLET – C | | | | | | | | | |
| EASTERN BLUEBIRD – U | | | | | | | | | |
| MOUNTAIN BLUEBIRD –V | | | | | | | | | |
| VEERY – C | | | | | | | | | |
| GRAY-CHEEKED THRUSH – R | | | | | | | | | |
| SWAINSON'S THRUSH – C | | | | | | | | | |
| HERMIT THRUSH – C | | | | | | | | | |
| AMERICAN ROBIN – C | | | | | | | | | |
| VARIED THRUSH – V | | | | | | | | | |
| GRAY CATBIRD – U | | | | | | | | | |
| NORTHERN MOCKINGBIRD – V | | | | | | | | | |
| SAGE THRASHER – V0 | | | | | | | | | |
| BROWN THRASHER – U | | | | | | | | | |
| AMERICAN PIPIT – U | | | | | | | | | |
| BOHEMIAN WAXWING – U | | | | | | | | | |
| CEDAR WAXWING – C | | | | | | | | | |
| NORTHERN SHRIKE – U | | | | | | | | | |
| LOGGERHEAD SHRIKE – V | | | | | | | | | |
| EUROPEAN STARLING – C | | | | | | | | | |
| WARBLING VIREO – V | | | | | | | | | |
| SOLITARY VIREO – U | | | | | | | | | |
| PHILADELPHIA VIREO – U | | | | | | | | | |
| RED-EYED VIREO – C | | | | | | | | | |
| GOLDEN-WINGED WARBLER – V | | | | | | | | | |
| TENNESSEE WARBLER – C | | | | | | | | | |
| ORANGE-CROWNED WARBLER – U | | | | | | | | | |
| NASHVILLE WARBLER – C | | | | | | | | | |

| CHECKLIST OF THE BIRDS OF QUETICO PARK AND THE ATIKOKAN AREA | | | | | | | | | |
|---|---|---|---|---|---|---|---|---|---|
| C = Common    U = Uncommon    R = Rare    V = Vagrant | | | | | | | | | |
| **SPECIES** | **DATE** | | | | | | | | |
| | | | | | | | | | |
| NORTHERN PARULA – C | | | | | | | | | |
| YELLOW WARBLER – C | | | | | | | | | |
| CHESTNUT–SIDED WARBLER – C | | | | | | | | | |
| MAGNOLIA WARBLER – C | | | | | | | | | |
| CAPE MAY WARBLER – U | | | | | | | | | |
| BLACK–THROATED BLUE WARBLER–R | | | | | | | | | |
| YELLOW–RUMPED WARBLER – C | | | | | | | | | |
| BLACK–THROATED GREEN WARBLER–C | | | | | | | | | |
| BLACKBURNIAN WARBLER – C | | | | | | | | | |
| PINE WARBLER – R | | | | | | | | | |
| PALM WARBLER – U | | | | | | | | | |
| BAY–BREASTED WARBLER – U | | | | | | | | | |
| BLACKPOLL WARBLER – U | | | | | | | | | |
| BLACK–AND–WHITE WARBLER – C | | | | | | | | | |
| AMERICAN REDSTART – C | | | | | | | | | |
| PROTHONOTARY WARBLER – V | | | | | | | | | |
| OVENBIRD – C | | | | | | | | | |
| NORTHERN WATERTHRUSH – C | | | | | | | | | |
| CONNECTICUT WARBLER – U | | | | | | | | | |
| MOURNING WARBLER – C | | | | | | | | | |
| COMMON YELLOWTHROAT – C | | | | | | | | | |
| WILSON'S WARBLER – U | | | | | | | | | |
| CANADA WARBLER – C | | | | | | | | | |
| SUMMER TANAGER – V | | | | | | | | | |
| SCARLET TANAGER – U | | | | | | | | | |
| NORTHERN CARDINAL – V | | | | | | | | | |
| ROSE–BREASTED GROSBEAK – C | | | | | | | | | |
| INDIGO BUNTING – U | | | | | | | | | |
| RUFOUS–SIDED TOWHEE – V | | | | | | | | | |
| AMERICAN TREE SPARROW – C | | | | | | | | | |
| CHIPPING SPARROW – C | | | | | | | | | |

**CHECKLIST OF THE BIRDS OF QUETICO PARK AND THE ATIKOKAN AREA**
C = Common      U = Uncommon      R = Rare      V = Vagrant

| SPECIES | DATE | | | | | | | | |
|---|---|---|---|---|---|---|---|---|---|
| CLAY-COLORED SPARROW – U | | | | | | | | | |
| VESPER SPARROW – U | | | | | | | | | |
| LARK SPARROW – V | | | | | | | | | |
| SAVANNAH SPARROW – C | | | | | | | | | |
| LE CONTE'S SPARROW – U | | | | | | | | | |
| FOX SPARROW – C | | | | | | | | | |
| SONG SPARROW – C | | | | | | | | | |
| LINCOLN'S SPARROW – C | | | | | | | | | |
| SWAMP SPARROW – C | | | | | | | | | |
| WHITE-THROATED SPARROW – C | | | | | | | | | |
| WHITE-CROWNED SPARROW – C | | | | | | | | | |
| HARRIS' SPARROW – U | | | | | | | | | |
| DARK-EYED JUNCO – C | | | | | | | | | |
| LAPLAND LONGSPUR – U | | | | | | | | | |
| SNOW BUNTING – C | | | | | | | | | |
| BOBOLINK – R | | | | | | | | | |
| RED-WINGED BLACKBIRD – C | | | | | | | | | |
| EASTERN MEADOWLARK – V | | | | | | | | | |
| WESTERN MEADOWLARK – R | | | | | | | | | |
| YELLOW-HEADED BLACKBIRD – R | | | | | | | | | |
| RUSTY BLACKBIRD – U | | | | | | | | | |
| BREWER'S BLACKBIRD – U | | | | | | | | | |
| GREAT-TAILED GRACKLE – V | | | | | | | | | |
| COMMON GRACKLE – C | | | | | | | | | |
| BROWN-HEADED COWBIRD – C | | | | | | | | | |
| NORTHERN ORIOLE – V | | | | | | | | | |
| BRAMBLING – V | | | | | | | | | |
| PINE GROSBEAK – C | | | | | | | | | |
| HOUSE FINCH – V | | | | | | | | | |
| PURPLE FINCH – C | | | | | | | | | |
| RED CROSSBILL – U | | | | | | | | | |

**CHECKLIST OF THE BIRDS OF QUETICO PARK AND THE ATIKOKAN AREA**

C = Common  U = Uncommon  R = Rare  V = Vagrant

| SPECIES | DATE | | | | | | | | | |
|---|---|---|---|---|---|---|---|---|---|---|
| WHITE-WINGED CROSSBILL – U | | | | | | | | | | |
| COMMON REDPOLL – C | | | | | | | | | | |
| HOARY REDPOLL – R | | | | | | | | | | |
| PINE SISKIN – C | | | | | | | | | | |
| AMERICAN GOLDFINCH – C | | | | | | | | | | |
| EVENING GROSBEAK – C | | | | | | | | | | |
| HOUSE SPARROW – U | | | | | | | | | | |

# SELECTED REFERENCES

- American Ornithologists' Union
  1983        Checklist of North American Birds.
              Sixth Edition

- Cadman, M. D. et al
  1987        Atlas of the Breeding Birds of Ontario
              University of Waterloo Press

- James, R. D.
  1991        Annotated Checklist of the Birds of Ontario,
              Second Edition
              Royal Ontario Museum
              Publications in Life Sciences

- National Geographic Society
  1987        Field Guide to the Birds of North America,
              Second Edition

- Peck, G. K., and James, R. D.
  1983        Breeding Birds of Ontario
              Nidiology and Distribution
              Volume 1:  Nonpasserines
              Royal Ontario Museum
              Publications in Life Sciences

- Peck, G. K., and James, R. D.
  1987   Breeding Birds of Ontario
       Nidiology and Distribution
       Volume 2:  Passerines
       Royal Ontario Museum
       Publications in Life Sciences

- Peruniak, S.
  1969   The Birds of the Atikokan Area, Rainy River
       District,
       Ontario, Part 1
       The Ontario Field Biologist
       Volume 23, 1969 (35 - 38)

  1971   The Birds of the Atikokan Area, Rainy River
       District,
       Ontario, Part 2
       The Ontario Field Biologist
       Volume 25, 1971 (15 - 32)

- Speirs, J. Murray
  1985   Birds of Ontario
       Volume Two
       Natural Heritage/Natural History Inc.

# INDEX TO SPECIES

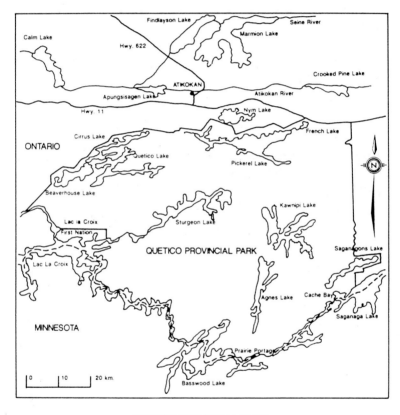

## QUETICO PROVINCIAL PARK

and the

## ATIKOKAN AREA